THE ONLY GIFT

ARNOLD · R · BEISSER

DOUBLEDAY

New York   London   Toronto   Sydney   Auckland

The Only Gift

Thoughts on the Meaning
of Friends and Friendship

PUBLISHED BY DOUBLEDAY
a division of Bantam Doubleday Dell Publishing Group, Inc.
666 Fifth Avenue, New York, New York 10103

DOUBLEDAY and the portrayal of an anchor
with a dolphin are trademarks of Doubleday,
a division of Bantam Doubleday Dell
Publishing Group, Inc.

Library of Congress Cataloging-in-Publication Data

Beisser, Arnold R.
   The only gift: thoughts on the meaning of friends and friendship
   by Arnold R. Beisser.—1st ed.
   p.   cm.
   1. Friendship. 2. Beisser, Arnold R.—Friends and associates.
I. Title.
BF575.F66B445   1991
158'.25—dc20   90-36019
CIP

This book is about and for my friends, and dedicated to the friendships they exemplify. Without them, my life would seem dull and empty of meaning.

CONTENTS

FOREWORD

THIS IS THE THIRD BOOK in the series that began with *Flying Without Wings.* In the first, I expressed my feelings about my disability. Next, in *A Graceful Passage,* I tried to get my feelings about death straight, since my age and extent of disability make my survival increasingly precarious and problematic. Now I come to something that makes my survival, with all of its attendant difficulties, seem worthwhile—my friends.

In trying to describe what a friend is, I asked some friends for their views, and sought to find how the English word "friend" had entered our language. How does friendship evolve, and how did I develop into a friend? The necessary skills to have a friend are not inborn, and so must be learned.

As I consider what some individual friends have meant to me, what I learned from each, and how our friendship developed, I began to realize that in each friendship the nature of the bond is quite mysterious, and what I believed to be the ingredients of the relationship might differ from what each of my friends believed.

So I asked those that I could reach to describe what our friendship had meant to them. And, indeed, what they had seen was not the same as what I had experienced. It made me wonder even more about the essence of this magic bond. Two people, connected in this mystic way, transcend the simple differences between people, and so the nature of this link may well hold the key to our survival as individuals, and for the whole of mankind.

I try to understand the place of "best friends" in the scheme of things, and how our views of good and bad can unite or separate us. Differences in sex may also play a vital role that cannot be ignored. Does money separate us, or cause us to unite with friends? And what about disappointments and betrayals? Can a broken friendship be repaired?

And what of time and friends? How long must you know someone to call him a friend? And, if time is important, is it ever too late to make a new friend? Does being separated by great distances terminate friendships, or can they be continued beyond both time and space?

These are among the questions I address, and I have tried with the information I know best—my own experiences with friends, and what they say of theirs with me. I try to summarize what I have learned about how to be and have a friend. And finally, I describe how in friendship we can discover our most critical connections with the whole universe, and the meaning of it all.

A book on friendship can best be done in concert with friends, as this one was. So I would like to acknowledge their contributions; however, in doing so I will mention only those few who had an active part. Although not mentioned here, every friend I have ever had, and everyone who has ever made a gesture of friendship in my behalf, is also somewhere in this book: if not by name, then between the lines, and in the beliefs I hold today.

To Jim Davy, Marty Weinberg, Helen Olander, Rose Green, Barbara Beers, Bud Blitzer, Jerry Jampolsky, Bob Derbyshire, Ted Myers, Hugh Prather and Frank Wood— a very special thanks for writing their thoughts about our friendship for me. To Clyde Wright, Don and John Echols, Fritz Perls, and Louise West, friends whom I have no way of contacting, I express my gratitude and good wishes, wherever you may be. Michele Biagioni helped me in many ways with the manuscript, and Dalia Blitzer prepared it for the publisher. Casey Fuetsch, my editor at Doubleday, skillfully guided the book through its development. And Rita, who is both wife and friend, has helped in many different ways.

The stories of friends included by name are to illustrate certain points, so I hope my friends whose names are not included will not feel slighted.

The only gift is a portion of thyself.
—RALPH WALDO EMERSON

ONE

What Is a Friend?

No man is an island, entire of itself . . .
—JOHN DONNE

THE CONTEMPORARY SAYING "People need people" is a way of expressing our need for association with friendly others. From birth to death we need the nurture of other humans, and nearly everything we do is affected by what responses we anticipate and receive.

However, family relationships and genes alone no longer determine who the significant people in our lives will be. More often today, they are not our family members at all, but people we have selected freely for a relationship. They are our friends.

Relationships are changing. People once lived in tight-knit geographically isolated groups, making it prudent to assume that those who were related by blood and lived nearby were the only ones it was safe to trust. It was naturally expected that strangers were generally up to no good. Thus ancient languages made no distinction between a stranger and an enemy; one word sufficed for both. Whenever a person encountered someone to whom he was not related or did not know, that person was automatically treated as a foe.

Mutual concern, intimacy, and kindness were reserved for one's own family and clan members. In fact, the very word "kindness" can be traced to "kin," meaning "blood relative." Thus kindness was reserved for family members and relatives. Because it was risky to offer kindness to an unrelated person or to a stranger, it was hard to be friends with one of them.

Languages change as new realities develop. Today, instead of as isolated tribes, we all live in a "global community." That means that we now must depend on others throughout the world—people who are not relatives—for the integrity of our environment, for the prevention of nuclear destruction, and for economic well-being. Moreover, each corner of the earth is now so readily accessible by mass communication and rapid transportation that strangers are not so strange anymore.

The pace of change seems to increase each day, spurred forward by new technology. We have instant news from around the globe. The electronic magic of telephones, radios, TV, computers, and fax machines brings information to us on everything, from everywhere. This information brings more change, making differences within family members greater, and generation gaps wider. So, with all of this ferment, people must rely more and more on friends.

The people with whom we live each day—work, play, study, plan, and travel, are more likely to have begun as strangers than as relatives. And we meet so many different people and have so many different opportunities that our choices have expanded too. As we move from place to place, from relationship to relationship, from job to job, often far away from home, we desperately need some trusted friends.

Our survival depends on finding ways to treat strangers and be treated by them with kindness, compassion, and benevolence—in short, as friends.

What, then, are the qualities of a friend? I know the feeling I have when I am with one. It is, "I belong here." Seeing a good friend is like going home, or like tasting Mother's cooking. I feel secure, and need not protect myself. "Here," I say, "it is safe, for I am loved."

The Oxford English Dictionary says a friend is "one joined to another in mutual benevolence and intimacy," and the word is "not ordinarily applied to lovers or relatives." Mutuality seems to be a key—the realization that your fate and your friends' are linked. That is a necessary part of friendship, but not enough to be complete.

"Friend" first appeared in Old English as "frēondum" in the classic work *Beowulf*, in A.D. 1018. The use and meaning of "friend" has changed and become enriched in the millennium that has followed. It is entirely possible for strangers to become friends, and be as close and familiar as any family member, something the ancients would have found difficult to understand.

However, it is not only the survival of our species that depends on our capacity for making friends, but our individual survival as well. Our cities are becoming unlivable because of what individuals do to each other. Residents are threatened by urban crime, random shootings, and other forms of individual violence. People who are in the way are treated as objects to be destroyed, no more than inanimate interferences.

And even when there is no threat of violence, we all still must be nurtured by caring others in order to give meaning to our lives. With the dispersion of our families and communities, nurturing is difficult to find. However, friends can provide the continuity in our urban landscapes; without them we would starve.

President Lyndon Johnson is remembered mainly for the tragedy of Vietnam, but his heart was in a "war on poverty." He wistfully observed that the world had become a neighborhood before it became a brotherhood. The challenge of today is to see if our neighbors throughout the world can become the brothers and sisters we would consider friends.

Yet, there is an important element of selfishness in all friendships, even if that does not appear to be so. We like our friends because of how they make us feel and because there is some mutual advantage to having them. Even in the apparent altruism of helping a friend, there is an element of selfishness, for in doing so I feel good.

I asked one friend for *his* definition of a friend. "Someone you can count on in a pinch," he quickly said. I asked another friend. "Loyalty," she said, with just as much certainty. Others mentioned consistency, sharing confidences, and thoughtfulness. "People you can do things you like with," another said. "Those who would never cause you harm no matter what," "unconditional love," "people who are like the part of you that you admire the most," some others said reflectively.

Trustworthiness is another quality that is prized. And honesty—"Someone who will tell you that your breath smells bad," one person wryly told me. Friendship then must transcend this paradox: "Be honest and do no harm." Yet that is precisely what occurs with friends, and if you know they sincerely care for you, you can accept the brutal truth. You know that what they say and do is with goodwill in mind.

An important thing about a friend is that he or she wants to be and share with you, without considering what material gain may accrue from the relationship. A confusing factor is that some people today are taught to act like friends, when manipulation is their only purpose. Salesmen of every kind are sometimes trained that way.

For example, although someone might try to appear a friend, it might be just to sell you a used car. They may try to show warmth and intimacy, but their intent is not benevolent, and their goal is just to make a sale. The concern they appear to show and the trust they seek are false, and so they do not qualify as friends at all. If you take advantage of a friend, you know you harm yourself.

The statue that stands in front of Father Flanagan's Boys Town depicts one boy carrying another. The caption beneath it reads, "He ain't heavy, Father, he's my brother." That is the way it is with true friends. They are no burden when you carry them—no more so than carrying yourself would be. The burden carried by a friend is yours to share, and your burden is also his, for you know your fates are linked.

Friends can accept and appreciate us for who and what we are, and for what we share—values, work, location, some experience, even other friends. We don't have to explain ourselves to them nor they to us. Friends know that in some basic way they are just like we are, and that is what allows us to become so close.

What, then, is the magical process by which a stranger becomes a friend? We need to look beyond the superficialities of manners, culture, and immediate design, for the ways in which we are all alike reside in a deeper layer. Beneath the surface, there is a potential friend in nearly every stranger.

We have been provided with the Golden Rule to guide us with our friends: "Do unto others as you would have them do unto you." What better place to start than that? Yet, even that must be qualified. For we need to look beyond what we would like to find with them. Sometimes Shaw's revision applies: "Don't do unto others as you would have others do unto you, for *they may have different tastes.*"

Empathy is a quality of friendship. Martin Buber has called the friendly bond an I/thou relationship. Friends are "thou's" instead of "its"—they are subjects, viewed the same way one does oneself, from the inside, instead of from outside appearances alone. If perceived only as an object, an "it," someone could just as well be made of stone. In empathic I/thou relationships, both people can fully show themselves, and can trust that it is safe.

When we are with a true friend—fully showing ourselves—our lives are elevated to a higher plane; for an instant we may know the view of God. For if He is really there, can He not view the world as each and every person does? As human beings, few of us can have that exalted view for very long, and rarely all the time. As close as we can come to Him is when we see the world as another does, even if it's only for a moment, with a friend.

And when we do, we become an *avatar,* like a god the Hindus say appears in different earthly forms. Although in temporal life an avatar appears quite ordinary, its human form embodies qualities that are divine. These transient incarnations descend to touch mankind with attributes beyond his base and selfish needs. Perhaps a true friend is an avatar who for a moment shows us that we can rise above our elemental atavistic nature.

To become a friend, we must show love; to have a friend, we must become a worthy friend—skills that must be learned. This book is my celebration of friends and friendships, relationships that each day grow more sublime. So I write first of how I grew and learned to be a friend, and then of those I call my friends.

My friends have their faults, as all of us do, but it is rarely what I see. Perhaps they hardly notice mine as well —I cannot say. We may see shortcomings in our friends, but we subordinate them to what our friends are at their best. Sometimes a friend will step upon your toes—but never with ill intent. And when in anger you strike back, it, too, is without malice, and designed to clear a path for love to appear again.

TWO

Learning to Be a Friend

Hand grasps at hand, eye lights eye in good friendship,
And great hearts expand
And grow one in the sense of this world's life.
                                    —RALPH WALDO EMERSON

RELATIONSHIPS come in many forms. There are fathers, mothers, brothers, sisters, grandfathers, grandmothers, aunts, uncles, cousins—all of whom are in the family to which we are born. We are assigned to teachers, bosses, coaches, and supervisors, where we are then divided as teammates, employees, peers, colleagues, and students. In all of these we have but little say.

But, ah, with friends . . . They are our choice! We alone determine who they will be. We can choose them freely from any who may have been assigned, or from any other place. It is entirely up to us and them.

My very first friends were adults who were, in many ways, like parents to me. But there were some very important differences. Next door there was Louise, a lovely young newlywed. I loved her blonde flowing hair and elegance, and I harbored secret desires for her I dared not feel at home. She, of course, treated me like the child that I was, but that did not keep me from wanting to marry her.

Learning to Be a Friend 13

And, next to our family bicycle store, there was Clyde, who had the shoe-shine stand in front of Billy's Barber Shop. He was as elegant as Louise, but the color of his hair was pitch black, and he wore it neatly slicked down. I especially liked the way he talked with me, more like a friend than an adult to a little kid. That made me feel very grown-up.

Were Louise and Clyde really my friends? Certainly not as my friends are today, but they were beginning relationships outside my family. What appealed to me was that being with them was different from being with my family, where I already had a secure place and behaved a certain way. Their lives were different from my family's, so a visit with them was an adventure. And what they said to me, and what I heard myself say to them, seemed different too. They were the aunts and uncles I never had, safe bridges to the world beyond my home.

Louise and Clyde were also ideals for me—how I would like to live when I was grown. They seemed all good, without a trace of bad, a way of seeing friends that I retained even later when my friends were peers. To see friends that way blinds one to their limits and faults, so later, when I was forced to see imperfections in friends, it was hard to know if they should remain my friends. Looking for models to admire may help you to improve yourself; however, it can sometimes also make it hard to be and have a loyal friend.

With utmost regret I must recall the times that I abandoned potential friends for insufficient cause: When forgetting their true worth, their failings were all that I could see; or, when they were disloyal to me, I failed to confront them with their deeds. I did not realize then that, as human beings, we are united as much by our frailties as by our virtues and our strengths.

When we are born we have no friends. They are not like families, where there is usually a ready-made place for us. We must earn our place with friends, and children are not naturally very good at it. The capacity to have a friend and be a friend evolves with time and the right kinds of experience.

Most of that early experience *does* take place within a family, and who is there and who is not makes a big difference in what can be learned. What happens with the individuals within the family provides the bedrock for future friendships, and establishes how much head start we are granted or how much we have to overcome to make friends.

Mine was a very small family—only my mother, father, my older brother, and me. I had no sisters through which to learn of girls, and no grandparents from whom to learn the past. Also, because we had no relatives who lived nearby, I did not know cousins, aunts, and uncles. Moreover, as newcomers to the area, there were no easy extensions of my family into the community other than those we forged ourselves. That perhaps explains how Clyde and Louise became so dear to me.

Before I could have a friend, I had to acquire enough personal autonomy to be able to move about and play, and of course be able to recognize a friend from a person who was not. Young children's minds cannot clearly comprehend what's going on, so when they get what they need, to them it's "good." And when they do not, it's "bad," and whoever made it so must be bad as well.

The good and bad that enter so early in a child's life soon merges with the family's unwritten rules of how its members should behave. Then, since the child's survival depends on remaining safely within the family fold, "in" and "out" usually also merge with "good" and "bad." In my small family those relationships were especially strong, since there was such unmistakable distinction between family and community.

It is difficult to keep your friends if every time you think they are good, they are "in" as friends, and every time you think they are bad, they are "out." Fortunately most of what I learned at home did apply to friends as well. However, I also learned that sometimes the unwritten rules my friends had learned at home were not the same as mine.

But that was not a problem with Don and John, the twins who lived next door. I cannot remember when we first began to play, for it seemed as though we always had done so. They were my first same-age friends and mine alone—not my family's, not my brother's, only mine. Then, one wintry day when I was only six, quite suddenly they moved away. Their father had been "transferred," we were told, as if by some mysterious unseen hand. I had done no wrong to justify this loss, nor had they. But still I felt the awful sense of it. That is when I first learned that when I am "in," and when I am "out," may not have much to do with what I have done.

Others moved into the neighborhood but none of them were like Don and John for me, my exclusive friends. So I dared not let these others get as close, and always held a little back for fear that they, too, might be "transferred" away from me.

Oh, of course, I played with them—cops and robbers, cowboys and Indians, we climbed trees and played with little soldiers and cars and trucks, and later there was Kick-the-Can, and we dug tunnels and built tree houses together. But I was just beginning to know the ups and downs of friends that made it hard to know if I was in or out with them, and if they were good or bad. So these new friends did not supply the intimacy I had known before.

It was not until I was in the fourth grade that I really found good friends again. Time, experience, and a new focus made it possible. It was sports that served as glue— softball, track, football, and especially basketball for me. We played together in school, at recess, after school, and every day in summer. Sometimes we were rivals against one another, and at other times we united to play against other teams and schools.

There was Dick, Tommy, George, and Wilson. But at the core were three of us—PeeWee, Robert, and me. Pee-Wee clearly knew the most about sports, and although he played with utmost zeal, he was not the best. Robert was the gifted natural, the fastest and most powerful. And I was somewhere in between.

Everything was action—practicing, playing, learning to be better. We competed fiercely and there were hierarchies in everything, especially in sports, but also in the classroom. We had pecking orders—who was fastest, tallest, fattest, most popular, and who excelled in each school subject.

Robert was best in arithmetic, PeeWee in spelling (except for Lois, who was the best in everything, but didn't count because she was a girl). Team positions in softball were not determined by special suitability, but rank order. That made Robert the pitcher, because he was the best player; PeeWee played first base because he was second best, and I was at second base because I was next best.

Robert was my best friend, PeeWee my second best, and each had their own rankings, and all of us talked openly about them. Best friends are important for kids at this age, for they are secure relationships outside the home, safe introductions to the larger world. Through them we learn that friends can be as close as family.

However, the world changes when we grow, as it did for us with junior high school and puberty. Robert, who had been very tall for his age, matured first, and then grew no taller. He became even more muscular, his beard sprouted; he discovered girls, and began pursuing them. He almost completely lost his interest in sports.

PeeWee had not begun to grow yet, so he did not improve much at sports, although he was still as interested. I grew taller, more awkward, and withdrew from girls, but threw myself even more zealously into sports. New coalitions formed, and the old gang was never the same again.

Although there had been at least ten small elementary schools in town, there were only two junior highs, one for the schools north of Main Street, the other for those south of it. I went south to Julia C. Lathrop. Many of the students there were the very ones I had known as opponents from rival elementary schools. They had been my enemies before, and now we were supposed to be friends, playing against new rivals.

I learned again how often the fates determine from whom your friends and foes are chosen. Accidents of geography and birth, in which we have no say, cast us together or apart. And more and more it becomes clear that you can find a potential friend in almost every enemy, and an enemy, if you wish, in every friend.

Marty, a rival in elementary school, a teammate in junior high, remains a loyal friend today. Linked by an ethnic destiny, my affinity with him has been a reflection of how I have seen myself. When I was alienated from that part of me, so was I from him, and as I have grown to trust and accept more of who and what I am, our friendship has also bloomed.

In elementary school I could not read very well, and was barely able to do the other classwork. But to my surprise, in junior high, schoolwork became a breeze. Sports still seemed the basis of my life, so my friends were

Learning to Be a Friend 19

also my teammates. But puberty made all of my relationships seem more tenuous. Girls were on my mind as much as they were with my friends, but in my confused awkwardness, I withdrew from them. I didn't know how to make friends with girls, and I felt alienated from guys who were preoccupied with talking to and about them—even dating.

When I entered high school, I did all I could to maintain my image as a jock. I would feign sleep and fool around in class to make it seem as if I did not care—the way I thought athletes should behave. Sports did continue to dominate my life, but the part of me that had withdrawn from girls and friends grew increasingly introspective.

I needed a good friend to share my thoughts and troubles with; however, I did not know what one would mean to me, or even where or how to look for one. That is when Big Jim appeared, and released me from myself. He showed me how to be and have a friend at this important stage in my life.

Perhaps most adolescents find friends more easily than I did. However, with each changing phase of life I needed to learn new rules for friendship and what the specialized opportunities for intimacy were.

Going to work, to college, and into the navy were the next big friendship opportunities. I was completely on my own for the first time, and that can be a very lonely trial. Fortunately, by now I had learned some things about how to find and make good friends without so much difficulty.

I had also learned that I could share when faced with common difficulties. Yet the most intimate of times occurred when we got away from problems—on days off, after finals, on leave, or liberty. We friends would share how hard it was, huddling together from the pressures of work or study, complaining about how irrational the military system was, and how we would make things work when we were in charge.

In college I was playing in tennis tournaments regularly. I met lots of people traveling and found fast friends; some have remained close all my life. For many people spectator sports have the same effect—as the partisans unite against a common foe.

Merwin was my doubles partner forty years ago, and although our lives have moved in many different ways, I know I can still count him as a friend. Dick, the best player of his time, still stays in touch. Tennis is even now central to both their lives, while for me it is like a faded dream. Yet, a bond remains.

Friendships at this stage seem to develop out of common trials faced in sport, work, school, or war. What I had learned before about friendship was useful then—to look for shared ideals, similarities for cooperation and competition in work and in play.

My friends seemed indispensable then, and as if they would last forever. However, when the common task is over, the friendships often also fade. How often I have heard men tell of the disappointment they felt in an anticipated later meeting with a best army buddy or college friend. With regret they discover they have grown in such different ways that nothing but the memory of the old camaraderie remains.

Because young men and women often vie for power and for each other, good and trusted friends usually come from the same sex. However, changes now are beginning to allow a greater range and freedom in sex-related roles. With sex itself more casual and defused, young men and women are becoming close and reliable friends more easily. But, tradition is still intertwined strongly with biology.

In the middle adult years, life revolves around solidifying career and raising children, so friends are made in the performance of these activities. They are met at work, because the kids are friends, or they have become your neighbors. If there is also some formal religious practice, that, too, may play a meaningful part, and weave your other activities together as a whole.

My wife Rita and I were not blessed with children, so our friends came from other sources. Most were "couple friends," who came from my work and from my past in school or tennis. Rita brought new friends from the neighborhood, tennis games, or civic involvements. When we got together, we would talk and eat, play games, and go to plays or movies.

We have a special group of friends that still endures, brought together by a common adversity. We call it our "polio group," since all the men were patients together in the same hospital after suffering the disease around 1950.

The men shared disability, and the women shared all they had to do to compensate. This has made us "couple friends." The bond is very strong and endures in spite of powerful and growing diversity—Catholic, Protestant, and Jewish faiths, arch conservative to ultra-liberal politics, and varying attitudes on almost every subject. Our similar ages, shared values, and interest in sports were the first attractions. Now, with almost forty years of history together, we are bound by time as well.

The men all managed to develop successful careers, despite their disabilities. Now, their children are grown and gone, retirement has either come or is imminent, and we are all facing declining energies and health. Two of the men have had heart bypass surgery. As we turn further inward, these enduring friendships become more irreplaceable and valuable.

When I no longer had an office outside my home, I sorely missed my friends at work. And I am sad to say that many have drifted far away. Fortunately some bonds are so strong that they do survive physical separation, as it has been with Bob and Helen, and some others.

Where are those friends of yesteryear? That is part of the mystery of friendship: it is hard to know which bonds will faithfully endure when others come and go; which are gone forever; and which may return at any time. When I have been in need of a friend, one usually has appeared—and from where, I could not foresee.

I do not have many close friends, just a few; but those I have grow more precious with each passing day. Although all the other friendship ingredients still exist, what grows increasingly important with the years is the support offered and received from them.

It becomes more difficult to develop new friends with advancing age, and those with history cannot be replaced. With those who have endured, there is no longer any need for explanation or proving myself, for I am known to them with all my strengths and weaknesses.

Yet, even so, the wondrous mystery of a friend still remains. A new friend appeared for me just the other day, and one I almost forgot I had just called. You never can tell when a friend will appear to fill a vital need.

I can never "have" a friend in the literal sense, because a human being cannot be possessed. Friendship is freely chosen, and that is what—in part at least—explains the excitement and wonder of the relationship. That also means that, to have a friend, you must truly be a friend.

THREE

First Friends: Louise

She walks in beauty, like the night,
Of cloudless climes and starry skies . . .
                                    —BYRON

MRS. MARSHALL was the owner of the house next door to ours on Garnsey Street. She didn't live there when I was growing up, but no matter who was renting it, we always called it Mrs. Marshall's house. The occupants I remember best were the Wests, a newly married couple. They were younger than my parents. However, Mom and Dad became good friends with them.

The Wests had arrived on Garnsey by a very different route than my family. They were descended from Orange County's most prominent families, and they seemed to inhabit a glamorous world well beyond our quiet neighborhood. Eddie, sports editor for the *Santa Ana Register,* was a dashing man-about-town, who was always busy. Louise was his beautiful wife who later became society editor of the paper.

Eddie was an impressive man himself—but, ah, Louise. She was the most charming and appealing woman I had ever met, and she became my first great love outside my home. She was slender and beautiful, always friendly and smiling.

Since she made it clear that she was fond of me, I used to spend time with her as often as possible, and would happily have moved into her house permanently, if I had had the chance. I liked to watch her as she worked around the house, and of course if we talked, that was even better. Although I always respectfully called her Mrs. West, I thought of her as Louise, the most beautifully euphonious sound I had ever heard. Watching her was a joy, and I took in her every move. Although I was only in the first grade, I secretly had plans to marry her.

Louise had a patrician-looking blond collie dog whose name was D'etre. Imagine that! Using a French term to name a dog. How sophisticated it seemed; our first dog was simply called Spot, and later we had one named Patsy. Louise tried to explain the significance of D'etre's name to me, but I could not fully understand it even years later, when I had some rudimentary knowledge of French.

D'etre was almost as lovely as Louise. Her narrow collie face and beautifully groomed hair were a great contrast to our mongrel Patsy, whose hind legs were grotesquely longer than her front legs. I was one of the few people to whom D'etre showed affection, besides Louise. With others, D'etre was as aloof as our Pine Street side walnut tree. How privileged I felt to have a place in the hearts of the beautiful D'etre and Louise.

The Wests' new LaSalle coupe was as splendid as they

were, and it had a rumble seat. Every Wednesday Louise would drive to Knott's Berry Place to buy some of Mrs. Knott's freshly baked berry pies for Eddie. She would invite me to accompany her, and when the weather was especially nice, she let me ride in the open rumble seat with D'etre.

At that time there was no bridge over the usually dry Santa Ana riverbed, so the road to Knott's was full of twists and turns, and ups and downs. How thrilling it was to ride in that rumble seat; these were my first roller coaster rides.

I was elated to be in the company of those beauties, Louise and D'etre, riding in the world's most beautiful car, with the cool breeze on my face. As we would pass farmers working in the bean fields and kids walking along the road, I would think how lucky I was, and how much they must envy me.

Louise had soft blond hair that she wore in a bun at the back of her head. One day, when I was visiting her, to my astonished eyes she opened up the bun and let her hair tumble down. It cascaded downward until I thought it might never stop, reaching well below her waist. As it unrolled, it released a delicate aroma that was like the orange trees in bloom. I had never seen or smelled anything like it before.

After that, each time I visited I hoped that she would let down her hair. Once I grew bold and asked her to. She reacted with mock affront, and gently scolded me. "Why, Arnold Ray Beisser!" she responded in feigned surprise. She always spoke my full name when she seemed to reprimand, and I loved that too, for there was no real insult there in calling me by my full name. Besides, I would rather be scolded by Louise than praised by most people. Although at the time I had no words for these experiences, they became a prototype for future relationships with women.

At Christmas the Wests would decorate their house in ways I had never seen. Their Christmas trees were cut on family lands. Of awesome size, they reached the ceiling, unlike the scraggly miniatures of other neighbors. I spent many joyful hours helping Louise decorate the tree, gravely selecting each ornament with utmost care. In the end it became a cornucopia of treasure displayed.

The angels and Nativity symbols were arcane mysteries to me, for our house was devoid of them. We decorated our small trees, gave presents, and sang "Jingle Bells" and Santa Claus songs at home, but there was no mention of what they meant or from where they came. No one had yet mentioned to me that I was Jewish.

At the end of 1931, when I was only six or seven years old, the Wests moved up to North Flower Street, into a big, new, beautiful home; the world was filled with bewildering surprises. There were more to come, but, oh, how I missed Louise, her hair, and D'etre, and how I missed those rides to Knott's in that marvelous rumble seat.

Later in 1932, D'etre made an unanticipated return alone. A major earthquake struck our town, leaving several people dead and more wounded. Everyone was terribly afraid that one of the hundreds of aftershocks might be an even bigger quake. The town's residents were warned to stay outdoors, so our whole family slept in Mom and Dad's 1928 Nash sedan for a week.

One morning, while sleeping in the car, I was awakened by a whining sound, and then a scratching at the car door. I rolled down the fogged window to see more clearly, and to my amazement, there was D'etre. Evidently she became confused, and returned to where she felt secure. She was terribly frightened, but was calmed by seeing me. I comforted her for a time, and gave her some food and water. She sparingly sampled them, and then we called the Wests to come for her.

Louise came in the LaSalle, and we had a brief, joyful reunion. Although D'etre preferred the rumble seat, Louise dared not trust her there in her frightened condition. After much coaxing from all of us, the nervous dog reluctantly jumped into the front seat alongside Louise. That was to be the last time I saw either of them.

Louise and Eddie kept in touch with Mom and Dad regularly by telephone for years, but the calls became less and less frequent, until there were none at all. Sometimes in town Mom and Dad would see them and talk, pledging to get together, but their lives were by then well beyond Garnsey Street. Eddie Jr. was born a few years later, Louise became society editor, and they never returned to the old neighborhood again. My only contact with the Wests was many years later, when Eddie interviewed me occasionally for the sports page.

Although the real Louise was in my life for only a brief time in childhood, her influence has remained with me, and the memory of her is still fresh. She was an ideal to me, the engram of an appealing woman. Only now in retrospect, do I realize that the girls who first attracted me possessed vestiges of her.

Friends are powerful influences in a person's life. "Birds of a feather flock together"; "He was a good boy until he fell among evil companions"; "If you run with trash, you become trash"—all express the view. And just as we unknowingly act in concert with the company that we keep today, those friends from long ago continue to exert *their* power, too.

Big Jim, whom you will meet soon, once said that seeing how well his friends had done was justification for him as well. What I believe he meant was that we look for in others what we can become—at best or worst. So it is wise to choose your friends with care, and be with those whose qualities you would like to share.

FOUR

A Model of a Man: Clyde

He was a gentleman from sole to crown . . .

And admirably schooled in every grace:
In fine, we thought that he was everything
To make us wish that we were in his place.
                    —EDWIN ARLINGTON ROBINSON

BEFORE I started school, I spent a lot of my childhood at the family store, Henry's Cycle Shop, so that Dad and Mom could watch me. But I did not have a useful place there, since everyone else was very busy working, and I was too young to help. Even my brother Stan, who was only three years older, could spoke a wheel, fix a flat, and talk to customers. But all I could do was to try to stay out of their way or tag along.

When he was not pressed for time, Dad would let me help him fix bikes, and if Bill, who worked at the shop part-time, was in one of his good moods, he would do the same. But if he was gloomy, I knew enough to stay out of his way. Sometimes, in desperation, I would even go out back to watch surly John painting in the shed. Most of the time I did not know what to do with myself.

My favorite hangout was the shoe-shine stand next door, in front of Billy's Barber Shop. This was Clyde's domain, and it was a wonderland, with people coming and going, always telling jokes and laughing. Sometimes they would whisper in his ear, adding an air of mystery to the fun. I loved Clyde, and I think Clyde loved me too. He never seemed bothered by my hanging around, although sometimes the men who came to see him looked askance at me.

The shoe-shine stand had brown wooden chairs perched on a platform several feet above the street, with removable wooden rests for men to put their feet on. It seemed like the crossroads of the world, and Clyde, its proprietor, seemed to know everybody and everything. It was a place of delicious mystery, excitement, comfort, and security where I learned how men behave.

I idolized everything about Clyde. He was the most impeccably dressed man I had ever seen. He always wore a suit with a white shirt and tie. His coat had always been removed, and was hanging on a hanger from one side of the shoe-shine seats. Only the tops of his shirt and fashionable tie could be seen, for the rest was covered by a spotless white or a pale blue smock. His lithe body and graceful movements could be seen behind the trim fit of his clothes, and were a marvel to watch.

His courtly manners were equally present with everyone, and he was as benevolent and cheerful with me as he was with Plummer Bruns, the mayor, or Mr. Howard, the chief of police. It seemed as if everybody in town knew and liked Clyde, and all dropped by to speak to him.

I could happily stand on the sidewalk for hours watching his smooth, easy movements as he shined shoes. He could improvise and create engaging rhythms with his magic shoe-shine cloth. When not engaged in conversation, he often whistled a little tune to the rhythms of the cloths. All the time he was transforming dull shoes to make them look spanking new.

His hair was never out of place. Combed perfectly, with regular waves, it was jet black and blended perfectly with his chocolate brown skin. It was the most beautiful hair I had ever seen.

Clyde was a man you could trust, and I knew that from my own experience. He would not tell on me when I did something I shouldn't have. He must have been trustworthy with everyone, for I often would see men speak with him in hushed voices, as though sharing a confidence. And although a shine cost only fifteen cents, a lot of one-dollar, five-dollar, and ten-dollar bills were exchanged, and Clyde always had a roll of bills that caused a bulge in his smock pocket. As the money was exchanged, they would huddle close to Clyde's little Philco radio, listening for results from Hialeah, Belmont, and Pimlico.

My mother and father were fond of him, and they always spoke of him as a "gentleman" and "educated." I had seen only one other black man in town, when he walked past the store going east on Fourth, to where I assumed he lived. Santa Ana and Orange County were predominantly white and Protestant, and people who were different stood out.

I was not aware of the ways in which Clyde's color affected his relationships with the people in Santa Ana, where life was filled with contradictions. Although he seemed to get along with everyone, and everyone seemed to like him, I can recall that he never went for coffee with the other men. I did not notice at the time, for from what I saw, it appeared that he was the most respected man in town—and in many ways he probably was.

The coffee break was a morning ritual among the West Fourth Street merchants. It went like this: about 10 A.M. Plummer Bruns left the McFaddin–Dale Hardware Store and crossed the street to our store—sometimes alone, sometimes with Mr. Howard, or with some other man. At our store he would stop and call, "C'mon, Henry, it's time for coffee."

Then they all walked towards the Ross Street corner, pausing briefly at the shoe-shine stand to talk with Clyde. Then they continued on to the Givens and Cannon Drugstore without Clyde. At the store, Charlie Givens would come out from behind the pharmacy to join the men at the lunch counter. Half an hour later the whole process would reverse. After stopping again to speak to Clyde, the men then dispersed to return to their respective places of work. It seemed so routine that I never thought to question why Clyde did not go with them—but come to think of it, I never saw him sit at the drugstore counter any other time either.

One of the delightful mysteries of visiting Clyde was that he kept an assortment of magazines for his customers, the likes of which I had never seen before. By far the most popular of them was *Esquire.* Most magazines of that period were printed on pulp paper like newspapers, with an occasional page or two of slick paper for special inserts. *Esquire,* however, was not only thicker and larger, but also printed on shiny slick paper throughout, and those pages contained the exotic mysteries of forbidden fruit. It was fiercely expensive; in the upper right corner was printed: $1.00—unheard of at a time when you could get *Liberty* magazine for five cents.

Beautiful photographs of the most advanced automobiles—Auburns, Cords and Pierce-Arrows—filled the pages. There were modern airplanes and skyscrapers, too. However, all of these were quickly leafed through to find the girls—pictures of the most beautiful women I had ever seen, with very little clothing on. There were the now famous erotic paintings of women in inviting postures by Petty and Varga. I devoured it all with my eyes.

Full-page color cartoons depicted apparently amusing off-color scenes of men and scantily clad women. Although I did not get the jokes, I knew that this kind of thing gave great delight to adult men. The height of adult fellowship for me was reached when, at Clyde's, the men would pass around some cartoon and exchange knowing smiles and snickers. So sometimes I would try to do the same thing with Clyde. "Take a look at this one, Clyde," I would say, and he would gently smile back. I, of course, did not get the joke in the cartoon, but it seemed like such a pleasant adult way to relate.

However, I noticed something strange—that when we were alone Clyde responded warmly to my adult mimicry, although when other men were there he seemed afraid, and disapproved. That puzzled me, but I began to dimly see that Clyde was not altogether free, and pictures of buxom girls, if shared with a little boy in the midst of lascivious men, was dangerous for him.

One other thing remained mysterious. I knew that Clyde lived in the back of the barber shop. That in itself did not seem so strange, because I knew that my parents had once lived in the back of our store. Neither did it seem strange that Clyde had never come to our house, for none of the Fourth Street merchants had. But I could see that living quarters were off limits, and as open and friendly as people were on the street with Clyde, there was a line beyond which he was not to pass.

Clyde had no gray hair, and his elegance seemed timeless. I would guess now that he was probably in his late thirties or early forties. I learned a lot from him about how to get on with the world, how to be respected by behaving in a graceful and understanding way. (Years later, as an enlisted man in the navy, I had another debt to Clyde, for I could shine my shoes for inspection much better than anyone else.)

I was used to seeing Clyde in the bicycle store, for he often came in just to visit. Sometimes he came to use the telephone, as there was none in the barber shop. But one day, when I was about seven or eight years old, he rushed in, looking as I had never seen him look before. The frantic way he moved and the expression on his face made it very clear that something terrible had happened. He paused in front of my father to say: "Mind if I go through your back to get to my room?" My father nodded agreeably, but sensing that something was amiss, added: "Anything wrong, Clyde, can I help?"

Clyde rushed past him and on out through the back, with these prophetic words trailing behind—the last I ever heard him speak: "My mother said, 'If you run with trash, you become trash.' " About an hour later two plainclothes policemen, whom I had known from the shoeshine stand, came in and asked my father if he had seen Clyde. Dad said, "Not since he walked through to the back, an hour ago." The two men questioned Bill and John as well, and then went out through the back.

My father went next door to see if he could find out what was going on. Billy the barber could not have been much help, for he seemed to have little awareness of much that was going on. Billy was an ancient man, I don't know how old, but he seemed to be the oldest person I had ever seen, and out of touch with everything.

My father was gone for a couple of hours, and when he came back, he looked awful. He went over and talked with my mother, and my mother's face dropped when he spoke to her. They both shook their heads, as though in disbelief. I knew enough not to try to find out what was happening just then, realizing that I would not be told anyhow. I went out several times to look at Clyde's shoeshine area, but it was closed, and all of his equipment was locked up tight.

That night, when we were having dinner, I asked my parents if anything was wrong with Clyde. Mom and Dad looked at each other, and then Mom said they would tell me later. After a long day's work at the store, they looked forward to quietly eating dinner with my brother and me, so they did not like to talk about anything unpleasant at the dinner table.

After dinner I was helping Mom with the dishes, and she said: "Clyde is dead." I was so stunned, I really could not comprehend—no one to whom I had been close had died before. My mother was willing to talk now, so I asked her more and more questions about what had happened.

She said sometimes young women from town would want to hang around with Clyde. However, he was very sensitive to how others might feel about a black man with white women, so he was very discreet. Only then did I realize that I had never seen women at the shoe-shine stand. My mother said that many people in town took a very dim view of any kind of social relationships between black people and white people, and Clyde was a person who wanted to protect his good reputation.

It seemed that two young high school girls came to Clyde and insisted that he take them to his room, threatening that, if he did not, they would tell the police that he had slept with them. Poor Clyde could see that they had him either way, and he could not win. He did not know if it was an idle threat, or if they really meant to do it. He evidently just decided to wait it out, until later he got word from someone in the police department that the girls had indeed filed a complaint. He must have figured that he was finished, so he came through our store to go around the back way to his room, where he had a revolver, and he shot himself in the temple and died immediately.

Clyde's mother came to take his body home and to collect his belongings. I didn't see her, but I can picture her in my mind from what my mother has told me. A small, frail, elderly black woman, who was well educated and dignified, had come for her son whom she had loved. She said, "He was always a good boy." She was a schoolteacher, and had attended university. We learned also that Clyde had had a year or two of college.

Dad was beside himself for weeks. One minute angry at the girls, then the police, and then at Clyde for not asking him to intercede. Then he'd be mad at himself: "I should have known, I could have done something," or even irrationally blaming poor old Billy: "Why didn't he know? He's too damned old!"

For months after Clyde was gone I would find myself walking out to the front of the barber shop to visit with him, and I'd have a wave of sadness and pain when I would see the empty stand. Several months later they simply dismantled it. I guess they knew, too, that there was no replacement for Clyde.

I have thought of Clyde and those tragic events many, many times. I would have thought that Clyde could have had the whole town as character witnesses, and yet, is it possible that people would have chosen race over friendship? And was the issue race at all, or was it that Clyde was reacting according to where he came from in the South?

And was the story just as I was told, or had Mom sanitized it for my child's ears? Perhaps more had happened between Clyde and the girls and, because they were juveniles, the penalties could have been severe. It's hard for me to believe that those men, the policemen, the judges, and other city officials who regularly visited Clyde, would have so completely abandoned him, but then I am often still amazed how quickly justice fades in the face of tribal solidarity.

It was for me the rudest shock, a fall from grace, that I still do not fully understand. He was innocent and so was I, yet that did not protect either of us from pain. Is every loss then a death that must be grieved? I had lost a friend I loved, and if that is not death, what is?

I know that parts of Clyde still exist in me, in my desire to always do my best and to live with grace. I can see it also in my desire to get along with everyone, in my capacity to accept what I may not like, and surrender to the inevitable. I know, too, like Clyde, that there are limits to all of these qualities, and that I would go to almost any lengths to avoid dishonor and disgrace.

FIVE

Time and Friendship: The Buddies

It is sublime to feel and say of another, I need never meet, or speak, or write to him; we need not reinforce ourselves, or send tokens of remembrance . . .

—RALPH WALDO EMERSON

DON AND JOHN ECHOLS were identical twins; they were also my two best friends when I was a child. Our birthdays were only a few days apart, so we were almost exactly the same age, and we lived next door to each other, making our friendship almost unavoidable.

Age and geography brought us together, and seemed to bond us forever. We spent nearly every day together, until they moved away in the middle of the term of our first grade in school.

I was Brother then, and they were known collectively as the Buddies. Individually they were Don and John, and although most people could not tell them apart, the differences were clear to me: John smiled more and was slightly smaller. But more than that, I simply knew them well enough to know that they were separate friends.

As soon as we finished breakfast in our respective homes, we met either at my house or theirs. We spent the days together until dinnertime. They were my first life with peers outside my home.

We played young children's games, I suppose, although I cannot recall what they were. One of us, either Don or John or me, would sometimes run home in tears. But later that same day, or early in the next, we were back together again, as close as ever.

Only once can I recall that we were divided along family lines, them against me. It was a rift so wide that we could not talk of it next day or ever again. In a shoe box they had proudly showed me a dead animal that they insisted was a squirrel. I was just as sure it was a rat. We argued back and forth until, pride at stake, they retreated home together in tears.

As I watched them go, I could feel my isolation reverberating with a distant memory—and then I knew my size had shrunk. It was like the lonely day I stared at Clyde's locked-up shoe-shine stand. That aching vacancy was antecedent to every future loss that I would know. Alone and small, all I could do was retreat, and try to find the safety I once knew at home.

Next day, although we were back together again, it was with a new wariness, for this squabble had injured pride, and was not forgotten as quickly as all the others had been. Although we were never clones again, we were now more realistically just best friends. And from that day on I knew I had to be careful in situations where someone's pride was at stake.

When we turned five, we began walking to Lowell School kindergarten together, each day carrying identical lunch pails. We were inseparable.

48   *The Only Gift*

We began first grade together, too, and sat one behind the other, all in a row. On the first day Miss Dudley read the roll, and then began to rearrange all seats alphabetically. When she saw the anguish that being asked to move caused us, she sensitively changed her mind and told us it was all right to stay right where we sat.

After only a few weeks in the first grade, our blissful unity came to an end. Clearly upset one morning, Don and John announced that they would be moving. I do not believe any of us really understood what that would mean, except that it was a disruption. They probably understood better than I, for they had moved before.

I remember the day the moving truck arrived, and all their family belongings were carted out. When it came time to say our good-byes they cried, but I did not. To me it seemed no worse than going home at night. I did not understand what moving would really mean.

However, I soon began to find out. I felt surprised to see that the next day they really were not there. It was only then that the relationship between the word "good-bye" and their really being gone began to have some grudging meaning. And when I had to walk to school alone, I felt strangely lost, and almost could not find my way.

I had no real words for my feelings. I remember my mother's vain attempts to reassure: "You are young, and you will have lots of friends." The words made no sense to me, for I did not care for lots of friends; it was Don and John I missed.

Time and Friendship: The Buddies 49

Only looking back do I realize how deeply I must have felt the loss. I went through all the expected motions at school and play, but the friends I met simply "did not take" with me; they were no substitute for Don and John. I must have been protecting myself from fear of another loss.

I retreated more to my special private world at home, and dared not show it to new friends. There is a blank within my memory for a year or two as it relates to friends, and it was not until the third grade that I began feeling attached to my peers again. And those I chose as friends had newly moved to town from far away—Robert and PeeWee. Perhaps, through some unfamiliar logic, I sensed in them the special friends I had lost.

Don and John may have briefly returned to visit once or twice, and I saw their grandfather, who continued to live nearby. But I do remember the Buddies clearly many years later, in the tenth grade. The Santa Ana High School basketball team on which I played traveled to play El Monte, where Don and John now lived.

I looked forward to seeing them, and they had wanted to see me, it seemed. At it turned out, I saw only one, for the other was sick at home that day. I think it was Don, but I could no longer easily tell them apart. I played in a different game than he, for I had grown quite tall and teams were arranged by the size of the players.

Nevertheless, we had some time together. We talked perhaps for twenty minutes or more, as long as we possibly could, until the bus pulled out for home. It was clear we had grown in different ways, but not apart.

Physically we were now very different: He was more compact and muscular; I was taller and leaner. He was more reticent than I, who talked a lot, but he seemed no less interested and involved. We both loved sports, and much, much more than that, we had both retained that indefinable link that had only been separated geographically, not in spirit. Although everyone else called me Arnold or Arnie, I was still, reassuringly, Brother to him.

Although we pledged to keep in touch, that was the last time I laid eyes on either of my childhood friends, the Buddies. But I did not forget them, and often wondered where they were. I tried to trace them once or twice in El Monte, but they were gone without a clue.

Thirty years went by without a word from them. I had reached my forties, and much had happened in my life since I last had contact with them. I had become paralyzed, I was a doctor, and I was married.

One day I was in my office when a call came. The voice on the other end was that of one of my long lost Buddies. "This is John Echols," he drawled in an unfamiliar accent of the Deep South. In spite of that difference, there was something in the voice I recognized, and that stirred something deep inside me.

Almost immediately we were engrossed in catching up on thirty lost years. We talked of what had happened in our separate and remarkably dissimilar lives. However, in another way, it was as though nothing had been lost and no time had passed. We seemed best friends again.

Don and John had moved to Alabama, where they both now lived. They had been air force pilots in World War II and afterwards went to the University of Alabama on the GI Bill, and married.

Both became owners of auto dealerships in southern towns. They had become pillars of their communities and true Sons of the Confederacy. They did not like to travel or leave home, and were in California at the time of the phone call for only a couple of days to attend a convention. They had traced me with considerable difficulty, just how I have now forgotten.

They were still alike in most ways, but now lived rather separate and individual lives. With me, it seemed that John was free to speak for both of them. We talked about many different things, for a long, long time. Soon, I began to feel much as I had when we were children. It was as if I had just gone home to sleep one night, and now, as usual, met with them the next day. Even though I was conscious that my work was piling up as we spoke, this conversation seemed far too important for me to cut off.

Although we did agree to stay in touch, we have gone our separate ways, continuing with our own lives. Nevertheless, I have not forgotten them, and still consider them to be good friends.

However, we are incongruous friends with very distinct

life-styles. They are southerners, and have been most of their lives, concerned with small-town business and politics. I live in a big city in the West, and my life has been in academia and medicine.

Our political, cultural, and religious beliefs probably separate us even further. We no longer speak alike, nor do our interests coincide. We had very distinct military experiences: they had been air force pilots in the thick of the fighting in World War II, and suffered many privations. Although I was in the navy both in World War II and Korea, I never even made it overseas. Yet they came out unscathed, while I became and remain paralyzed.

Just as we now speak with different accents, so have our lives been accented differently. There is much in them I do not know. We have not shared our triumphs or our failures. I do not depend on them, nor they on me. And when I think of my close friends today, they would not be among the first by far. Perhaps we have not stayed in touch for fear that further closeness might endanger what we still have and value. I cannot say for sure.

I know our bond has not endured any great stress or test in recent years. Yet there is something that has sustained more than thirty years without any contact to reinforce it. Something fundamental has remained the same, and the bond that was formed in childhood is yet unbroken. They care about me, and I for them.

Just to have remembered that we had been friends would be remarkable enough, for our physical relationship ended when we were six years old. But this was a good deal more than that; I know I felt that special warmth of stable friendship when we talked.

Thirty years without association, and yet something remained the same! Perhaps that *is* the nature of what we call true friendship—that it touches something timeless, deep inside, something undisturbed by petty and mundane affairs, something with a power of its own, something more than you or me.

To say that this bond is simply fond memory or nostalgia does not explain its feel or intensity. There is much more here.

After my book *Flying Without Wings* was published, I heard from other long-lost friends. What a joy that is for me! I heard from Jack in New York, and Ann and Barbara, too. Jim and Marty, my dear old friends, arranged a book party for me in Orange County. I saw lots of friends I had not seen in half a century—including Kearney, Max, and Nancy from my kindergarten class!

I even heard from Junior Clark, who called from Memphis, Tennessee, with an accent as deep as Don and John's. He said, "This is Randolph Clark," but I knew it was Junior right away. He reminded me that his address had been 318 South Garnsey, and mine was 315. "That close," I thought, for his house seemed very far away.

Perhaps that provides the clue to why these old and distant friends still seem so close. The world was very small when I was young. So everyone within it seemed very large and important as well. Yet the wonder is that, while the scope of my world has now grown enormously, the sanctity of friends new and old has also grown even more, strengthening my feeling of connection with all of life.

SIX

Learning Again to Be a Friend: Big

We love those who know the worst of us and don't turn their faces away.   —WALKER PERCY

WE CALL HIM BIG NOW. It was Big Jim in high school, where he was the tallest, if not the best basketball player on the team. However, that is the least important way in which he was and continues to be big.

He believed in friends. He taught me about friendship and how to have and be a friend. He invited me to share my private world and showed me it was safe to do so. He did not wait for me to begin. Big Jim never was known for his restraint. He always dove right in, no holding back.

It was our first year at Santa Ana High; we had come from different ends of town, and so from different schools. We met in study hall.

I had an acute case of puberty and adolescence when I began high school, and it had driven me underground. On the outside I acted cool and competent, and assumed everyone saw me that way, for I was a good athlete and did all the right things. But I knew it was a facade, and inside I often felt so nervous, I thought I might explode. I felt ashamed of all my doubts, afraid and very much alone.

We were acquainted only casually when one day he stopped me as I was walking out of study hall. Out of the blue he said: "What's with you? You're a pretty popular guy, but you don't seem to have any real friends." I was shocked to hear what I dared not admit myself. How could he know? After all, I hung around with lots of guys and seemed to do all the right things.

I mumbled something incoherent, like naming all my superficial relationships, to get him off my back. But he was sure of what he'd said, and just ignored my ploy. "Friends are the best things you can have, you know." I knew he was right, and although I was acquainted with a lot of people, they were not my confidantes or intimates.

Something in his manner let me see this was not attack, not criticism, not preaching, just plain interest in who and what I was. That is the way with Jim—no subterfuge, no guile, just openly coming straight to the point, telling how things look to him—even if it often gets him in trouble.

That kind of honesty compels a response in kind, and I could not resist the invitation he implied. Soon, almost before I knew it, I was sharing hidden parts of me with him—nothing special for an adolescent, but they were things I had feared to say. And what relief it was to share at last those private shameful thoughts of lust, fear, and confusion.

I felt inadequate with girls, and was relieved to learn that the girls who nearly drove me mad (concealed beneath my mask of cool, of course) had the same effect on him. And I was not alone in my fearful thoughts, my rebellious ideas, and various other secrets. We had found different means of handling them; Jim barreled ahead, while I had turned inward.

And that was that, the bond of friendship forged. Throughout the rest of high school we were best friends, we talked of everything for hours on end, from idle gossip to the meaning of life—girls and school and girls and the future and girls and politics and girls and Santa Ana and parents and ambitions and fears—and girls, of course.

In high school I did not date very much, for I could not reconcile being cool, as I tried to be, with all the inner anxiety, fear, and doubt I felt. Jim was more adept than I, but not so far ahead of me that he could not understand how and what I felt.

Even then, Jim had great integrity. Dishonesty was alien to his every way, and that had great appeal for me. He was always candid—he could be no other way—and he usually knew what his position on any issue was. In this he was my teacher.

I did some things with Jim that I would never have tried alone. One long weekend, for example, we hitch-hiked a thousand miles to Berkeley and back, in the rain, to visit our brothers. Sometimes, in a major act of rebellion, we would quietly drive along sidewalks and house lawns in the early hours of morning. When he drove, it was in my neighborhood, when I drove, it was in his. Luckily we never encountered any neighbors or pedestrians.

He forced me to face some personal conflicts between my social duty and personal responsibility. When he ran for student body president on the anti–service club party, I was president of one of the clubs. As such, I was obligated to run the campaign of a rival candidate.

My dilemma was how to support my best friend, Jim, and still carry out my social obligations. I had to think long about it, and my resolution was to vote personally for Jim, and campaign for his opponent. This probably is not what I would do today, but it was my best solution then. (Oh yes, Jim won the election.)

Most of the time we were on the same side, as when a popular teacher was summarily dismissed without any explanations. We were incensed. To protest, we got every student in school to sign a petition asking for reinstatement.

The principal, Mr. Crawford, got wind of the petitions before we could submit them to the board of education. He coldly summoned us to his home on a Sunday afternoon where he excoriated us for meddling in things that were, to him, none of our business or concern. He demanded that we turn the petitions over to him. He succeeded in confusing me with his wrath and righteous authority.

When we left him, I was uncertain what to do. We talked it over, and here is where our versions of the event are very different. I remember that it was Jim who retained his resolve, in spite of the principal's threats and intimidation, and then he convinced me that we should still send the petitions to the board of education.

In Jim's version, it was I who resisted the principal's coercion and convinced *him* that we should go ahead with the plan. Each of us, thus, thought the other was supplying the necessary strength and courage to complete what we had planned.

And that illustrates an important principle I have learned about friendship: Two friends are together much more than the simple sum of both. They form a stronger, more understanding and compassionate being than either person is alone.

Neither Jim nor I supplied the necessary courage to carry out our task. It was, instead, that we were together. With the bond between us, we each possessed more fortitude, strength, and spirit.

It is as though two friends can form a third entity that has a greater human capacity than either individual, even working together. If, alone, each possesses a capacity of one hundred human units, we might expect no more than two hundred from both of them together. Surprisingly, though, together they may develop much more than that, more like four or five hundred.

That must be why so many great and terrible human acts are done by pairs or groups. One person usually gets the major credit or blame; but without the other, far less would have been done, for good or evil. Clyde Barrow acting without Bonnie Parker would not have been as bad, neither would Hitler without Goering. And Schweitzer and Gandhi without their loyal friends would not have accomplished so much.

This does not mean that good friends are only that third entity. Jim and I have always had our individual views on many issues, just as in the matter of the high school election, and each of us has felt free to act alone. We haven't *had* to give in to the other. But still we formed something more than simply him and me—a third being that could show us a way with more fortitude, more boldness, and more resilience.

As it turns out, we did take the petitions to the school board, but we were ignored and nothing came of it. Well . . . almost nothing. Jim and I had convinced a classmate named Barbara to circulate the petition for the junior class. I was secretly in love with her, but far too shy to speak on my own behalf. However, I could act for the teacher I believed had been maligned.

We overlooked one distressing fact: Barbara's father was superintendent of county schools, and the awkwardness that developed became the prototype for all my future romantic efforts with her. Although her father never said a word, her mother treated me very coolly afterwards. Barbara and I could never quite seem to get together after that.

But these events only strengthened my relationship with Jim, and I have no better friend in all this world— there is so much of him to love. His openness and candor continue, as do his thoughtfulness and concern. Recently Marty, whom you will meet next, and Jim and I attended our forty-fifth high school class reunion with our wives.

Elaine, Marty's wife, who is quite active in politics, was intently talking to a classmate who now holds elected office and who, as a Latino, often represents the Spanish-speaking community. He was pointing out to Elaine how few of the Mexican students in our class had come to the reunion, because they would feel unwelcome, just as they often had in school.

To further illustrate his point, he was in the midst of observing that hardly anyone at the reunion knew his name. Just then Jim walked up and said with his usual directness, "I can't recall your name." The two politicos laughed very hard.

Jim, however, was much chagrined when he was told the substance of the joke, and was filled with concern that this indeed implied a prejudice in him. The Latino representative was not offended, for he knew Jim. And none of us, after forty-five years, could remember many names, although most of us played along as if we did and waited for clues in the conversation. But not Big Jim. He is always candid, always open, but never cruel or insensitive. And he applies those qualities to how he sees himself as well. He is always ready for self-examination, and willingly takes responsibility for his actions. There are some elements of prejudice in all of us, but in Jim far less than in most. His integrity insures an open hearing every time.

When I became paralyzed, there was disruption in

many of my friendships. With Jim a continuity existed, for which I can't claim responsibility. I was angry, blaming, and depressed. It was Jim's persistent caring and accepting attitude that made the difference.

He has always been aware of my special needs, and automatically responds to them—carefully noting wheelchair accessibility to places, anticipating how I am to be situated, and offering any help that I might need—all done unobtrusively.

His helpfulness has created some quirky scenarios that still can make us laugh. Once Jim wanted to give me a ride in his speedboat. He and a friend decided the best way to get me in was in dry dock, and once I was on board, they would launch.

All went as planned until the boat hit the water; then they watched in astonishment as it slowly began to sink, with me alone on board. They had forgotten to plug the drain! I began to softly sing "Aloha," as the water rose around me. Swift action by those on shore brought the boat and me back on dry land before any harm was done. But the memory is still a source of much amusement.

As the center of my small world, I have described Jim from my standpoint, perhaps giving a narrowly distorted view of his accomplishments. Although he has many, many friends, there is much more to him than that. With his wife Phyllis they have produced three fine children, now all grown, married, and successful. Until a few years ago Jim was president of one of the largest newspaper advertising companies. Now semiretired, he has returned from New York to Orange County and has begun his own newspaper syndication company. He was even active in local politics, at one time mayor of his city. And he always finds time for his friends.

SEVEN

Avoidance and Affiliation: Marty

Be slow to fall into friendship; but when thou art in continue firm and constant. —SOCRATES

O N THE CABINET in my bedroom is a framed snapshot taken of a group of little kids at a birthday party as they stand awkwardly posing for this grown-up interruption of their fun. It is the earliest visible evidence of my relationship with Marty, taken at his seventh birthday celebration.

In the photograph Marty is uncharacteristically somber, but still looking as handsome as he does today. I am squinting against the sun, while my brother glumly towers over me from behind. Our expressions make clear that posing for the camera was an undesirable intrusion into the party festivities.

Ours were among the small handful of Jewish families in Orange County and, although our families were never close and we attended different elementary schools, it seems as though I have known Marty all my life.

I had mixed feelings about being Jewish. In fact, I did not know that I was, until I was about five years old. In our neighborhood lived a high school football star and his sister. All the little kids hung around their house in admiration.

One day when I was visiting there, the sister said to me: "You know, you are pretty cute for a little Jew." Although I did not know what a Jew was, the implication sounded clear, that it was something to be overcome. I went home perplexed, to ask my mother what being a Jew meant.

I do not remember what she said, but it could not have been enough to dispel my concerns, for I grew up with ambivalent thoughts and confused feelings about my heritage. I felt loved at home, and fortunate to be part of our small close-knit family, but I retained a vague sense that I should be wary of how others would regard me.

Orange County was an unusual place with regard to ethnic and racial differences, for people lived in comfortable contradictions. Then, as today, the region had an image of bigotry and ultra-right-wing political activity. The Ku Klux Klan held its national convention in Anaheim when I was young, and other racist groups had strongholds there.

Yet, although there was organized opposition to groups with cultural differences, at the same time there was a remarkable degree of tolerance and acceptance for the individuals who were a part of them. My parents were on best of terms with people who could despise Jews as a group.

Once, a man came to my father to report that another mutual acquaintance had called him a dirty Jew. Dad answered without rancor that, as far as he knew, he was not dirty, but indeed he was Jewish. The stunned man just stared at him in disbelief, then stammered: "But, Henry, you are my friend and the nicest guy I know; you can't be a Jew." Dad confirmed that he was. The man thought a long while, and at last the light of discovery came into his eyes. Having solved the problem, he said: "Oh, you must be a white Jew!"

Now it was my father's turn to be confused. "What's a white Jew?" he asked. "Oh," the man answered, pleased with himself, "that's a good one, like you." The human mind is wonderful in its capacity to find relief by rationalizing contradictions.

The man was a successful political official, kind and effective, but he reflected the prevailing community attitudes that were filled with contradictions. Of course there were a few hard-core bigots in town, and there were limits to the general attitude of tolerance. The tragic events with Clyde powerfully illustrate that.

If a minority group is small, it poses little threat to a community; if it is large, however, the prejudice grows. So in Santa Ana, although Catholics, Jews, and Armenians were treated mainly as individuals, Mexican-Americans were not. There was organized discrimination towards them, and they lived in two ghettos—one at the northern edge of town, the other, south in Delhi.

Although my family certainly did not harbor resentment toward Mexican-Americans, I was also a child of my community, and, sometimes, I reflected its prevailing attitudes. So I was not at ease with being Jewish, and I considered Marty with the same ambivalence I did myself. Yet, while I was in a quandary about what being Jewish meant, to my surprise he seemed quite proud of it, and he seemed like "a regular guy," good at sports and popular —the values of the time.

However, I saw him only rarely. He did not live close by, and I attended Lowell Elementary School; Marty went to Spurgeon. Spurgeon, in fact, was one of our biggest rivals, and softball determined the fiercest athletic rivalries. (The sport was far more important than baseball in Orange County in the days before major league baseball came to the Pacific Coast). I knew I would see him when our teams played.

When Spurgeon took the field against us, Marty was their center fielder. As they warmed up, I watched him with a cautious eye to see how good he really was. They called him by the nickname Mitts, which I took to suggest "butterfingers," assuming he could not catch well.

Since in some vague way our fates seemed linked, a nickname that implied vulnerability for my friend would have to affect me as well. I felt incoherently uneasy as the game began, but I quickly forgot my anxiety as I became absorbed with winning. Our team had come to win. We were the good guys; they were bad guys. No room was left for kinship with the opposition.

PeeWee Power, our lead-off man, opened with a walk; I followed with a single, and by the time our half of the inning was over, we led 3 to 0. We continued to run up the score, but it was in the third inning that an event occurred that I still remember vividly. Our cleanup man, Robert Barrett, hit a high fly ball into centerfield, where Mitts was playing. As he chased it, I could feel anxiety grow; two mutually exclusive thoughts collided in my head.

For our team to win, I wanted Mitts to drop the ball and assure our victory. But I wanted just as much for him to make that catch, because a part of him also seemed like me. Two contradictory impressions and two desires: my allegiance to my school against a part of who I was. Our team must win! Mitts must look good! So my dilemma grew as the ball completed its graceful arc.

I discovered that my definition of his nickname was wrong. Mitts implied proficiency at catching, as I saw when Marty casually floated back and deftly pulled it into his glove. He rifled it into second base to hold our man in check. That catch reassured the part of me that lay in Marty's hands. The rest of me was relieved our team was also still ahead—so I had won on both accounts.

It was not until that night when I lay in bed that I could sort things out, and it has taken years to truly understand what I described. However, we had won, all of us, the team from Lowell and the part of me that was contiguous with Marty.

After elementary school, Marty and I both attended Lathrop Junior High, where I first began to know him fairly well. We both played every sport, and were on the same basketball, football, and track teams. We played for

Scotty's Malts in the summer softball league. I continued at second base, and Marty still roamed in center field. We even ran against each other in a school election for "student body judge," and, to my dismay, Marty won.

Although we were now together as teammates and friends, we were never really very close. I wanted to belong and felt that being Jewish set me apart. I was bothered as much by the stereotype that Jews were intelligent as by the one that they were untrustworthy. What I wanted to avoid was being different. So when Marty proudly proclaimed he was Jewish, I avoided him. The distance that I kept from him was the distance I kept from the problematic part of me. To be a real friend to Marty would have required that I accept more of myself, something I was not yet ready for.

How little I could see outside myself! For if I had, instead of stereotypes I would have seen what I do today in Marty, a thoroughly admirable person—a generous, kind, and faithful friend. My relationship with him has been a reflection of the degree of my acceptance of myself. Perhaps that is the way it always is with friends. Those who are most accessible to friendship also are more at ease inside themselves, and one state creates the other. Could we be a friend to everyone if we could just tolerate ourselves?

When Marty and I entered high school, we still played on the same basketball team and had a few classes together. But in other ways, we went our separate directions. The distance between us came, in addition to the ambivalence I felt about our common ties, from my discomfort with girls, and all the associated dating activities. I was still too shy to even talk with or about them, while to Marty it seemed a breeze. Our main connection, then, was through Big Jim, our mutual friend.

When we graduated from high school, the cataclysmic events of World War II were at their peak. We all knew we would soon be in the thick of it. In my yearbook, Marty, who always held a noble, almost naive patriotism, wrote this prophetic statement: "Now we must do our share for Uncle Sam; I will be doing my part very soon."

And indeed he did his part and more. As an infantry private, he landed at Anzio beachhead in the thick of battle. His company suffered enormously high casualties against the Germans as they fought their way north along the Italian boot. Marty was wounded in a fierce battle near Bologna.

He spent months and months in military, then veterans' hospitals, enduring operation after operation, to mend a badly damaged leg. It never fully healed, and has continued to be painful, requiring more surgery. Sometimes his limp is quite pronounced, but he almost never complains or speaks of it. And that is one of his many appealing qualities: He does not speak ill of others, and he does not complain.

Unlike most of us, Marty's appearance has kept pace with his accomplishments. He always dresses impeccably, a fitting accent to his still youthful form. He has not lost a single hair, and now that it has turned white, he is the very model of a "man of distinction." Even his limp does not detract, but instead seems to add a bit of mystery to his visage.

During the three years I was hospitalized with polio, Marty visited me with Elaine, who would become his wife. However we still had very limited contact until after I was released from the hospital, returned to work, and was married. Then, we began to visit each other as couples.

Now I was able to see him more clearly and appreciate him for who he was rather than what he represented to me. And in a strange way, becoming disabled cleared my view and gave me more perspective on what things were important and what was not. I had to revise who and what I thought I was and that had to include all of me.

When Big Jim retired to Orange County, the three of us began to see more of each other. We went on vacations together with our wives several times and occasionally still get together for dinner. The relationship between Marty and me has flourished beyond just our association with Jim. There are many things we do together and we have shared confidences that no one else knows. I get a special pleasure when I can be of use to him, and I think the same is true for him.

There is no better evidence of how close we are now than that we are open about our differences. Recently I became angry at him, and told him. Elaine became involved as well, and for me it has made clear how much a treasure they both are as friends. Is that not the ultimate test of friends, that the wonder of the relationship reduces conflict and differences to triviality?

Now Jim and Marty drive to my house in West Los Angeles each month for lunch. Often they will bring other old high school friends. It is not an equal arrangement, for it takes them three or more hours' driving time to spend about three hours with me. I feel bad that I don't do my share of traveling, but they do not complain, and insist it's more than worth the trouble. That is true friendship, with Southern California traffic what it is!

We talk about most everything, including our perceptions from the past. Each time we meet, I rediscover some lost pieces of myself.

But something important is missing from this description of my relationship with Marty. I cannot quite put my finger on it—it defies words—but it goes deeper than only our ethnic connection. I think that I have always had a linkage with him, even at times when we were not close. An essential human dilemma has been manifested here: While we each function individually, we are also united and as one, and I have felt that in my relationship with him.

Marty and I grew up together, and yet apart. Now we grow ever closer, and share what has been hidden from view. We originally were brought together by a past we had no part in designing. Now we have freely chosen to come together as enduring friends. I know he loves me now, as surely as I know I love him.

EIGHT

Jerry Jam and His Jamborees

I love everything that's old: old friends, old times, old manners, old books, old wines . . . and old friends are best! —OLIVER GOLDSMITH

IN MEDICAL SCHOOL I expected to share a room with a fellow student I knew from college. However, when we arrived, we found we had a room for three instead, and we considered the extra man to be an unwelcome intruder. We showed our unhappiness by treating him icily. Although he was clearly hurt by our actions, he made no protest. He seemed to be without a capacity for malice, almost too gentle and accepting for his own good.

However, malice was not in short supply elsewhere in the competitive climate of medical school. He became the object of much of the accumulated hostility within our class. Tormentors were incited by his accepting gentleness, almost as though they had to test its limits.

When he walked down the hallway, he was likely to be tripped. Because he was known to sleep so soundly that he would awaken confused, one night he was deliberately awakened, and a live bird placed in his unsuspecting hand. The confused terror produced by this sadistic prank created gales of satisfied laughter amongst the perpetrators, and it remained a topic for their amusement for weeks.

Spurred by the success of these and other pranks, the merrymakers organized the class to participate in alternating days of hate and love for him. On days of hate he was treated coldly, and almost no one spoke to him. Then on days of love, he was showered with effusive and overly dramatic displays of affection. Both the coldness and the insincere affection caused him pain and consternation.

But he was no mere dupe and certainly no fool. At the very same time that these cruel events were occurring, he was also regarded with utmost sincere affection and uncommon trust. Among the students, it was to him that fellow students turned in times of need, for he was an ideal confidant. Whatever it was that made him vulnerable to malicious antics had also given him a depth of accessibility and understanding to all that was within the human soul.

His goodwill was a magnet for strong emotions of every kind, and they seemed to accompany him wherever he went. Jerry Jam and His Jamborees, the name of a dance band he had organized in high school, was how I thought of him and our classmates when involved together.

At the end of our first academic year we had a welcome three-month vacation. One evening a group of us sat together discussing our plans. Most were preoccupied with finding work to help pay expenses for the next year, while the more affluent contemplated exciting travel plans. To the guffaws of all, Jerry, who needed to work as much as any of us, declared his intention to find a way to combine both. For even then, he believed in miracles; anything was possible.

Next morning, not in the least discouraged by the skepticism that had been expressed, he took the cable car to San Francisco's most exclusive men's club. Unnoticed by the guard at the door, he followed a member into the sacrosanct clubrooms. Once inside, he approached a distinguished-appearing member, politely introduced himself, and candidly explained his mission.

Astonished by his hubris and not knowing what else to do, the member took him to the manager, who berated Jerry for trespassing, and threatened to summon the police. Jerry calmly repeated his purpose to find a high-paying job that would also provide him with an interesting travel opportunity. This, he naively explained, would prepare him for the rigors of the next year's medical studies with both money and respite.

The manager was completely disarmed by his arresting candor, and instead of summoning the police, called a member who was the president of a major cruise ship line. The president was equally captivated by the young man's guileless manner. A few days later Jerry was informed that a new position, as doctor's assistant, had been created for him on a luxury liner that traveled continuously between Honolulu, San Francisco, and Los Angeles. To the amazement of his classmates all that summer, and each vacation from medical school thereafter, he cruised. Oh yes, of course, the job paid very well, too.

And by the end of this first year, this former "intruder" in my life had become my closest friend. The next year we were roommates and shared jobs as "hashers" for our meals. After that we moonlighted together at a hospital to support ourselves until we were graduated.

Sometimes I was the beneficiary of his charmed life. We had barely enough money to manage to rent a tiny furnished room in a boarding house, when one day Jerry announced another miracle, that he had found us a fine apartment for less than what we now paid for our dismal room.

When I first saw it, I could hardly believe my eyes. It was indeed large and tastefully decorated, with an attractive fireplace—perfect for the parties and dates for which we had no place before. The affordable price was unbelievably low.

The catch was that this was a basement apartment in a very unusual building. All of the other people in it were gay. Today this probably would have less unnerving significance. However, although we considered ourselves sophisticated medical students, this was the forties, and we were very naive by today's standards. All sexuality was more mysterious then, and we filled it with our prejudices and fears. Nevertheless, the appeal of fine accommodations outweighed our fears, and we moved in.

And it proved to be an enlightening experience that defied most of our prejudices. We had good and thoughtful neighbors who expected nothing more from us than that we pay our rent. We also got a sense of what it must have been like for them, for we were the minority there, and occasionally an embarrassing situation would arise when a visitor assumed that we, too, were gay.

Upon graduation, Jerry followed a conventional medical pathway. Psychiatry had always been his choice of fields. He married, had two fine boys, and developed a successful practice. He lived in a style befitting the prominent status he had acquired.

For the next twenty years, this was the basis for his life. Yet there was something in him that remained unfulfilled, something that yearned to be expressed. The signs of it appeared from time to time, and he seemed to lurch between painful disaster and miraculous good fortune, while seeking his true destiny.

Accidents and fires seemed to plague his life, and sometimes he may have drunk too much. Yet he also began a free children's center, where he gave of himself generously while providing helpful services to children and their families. The dualities of his life that I saw first in medical school demanded more expression and integration as time went by.

When his marriage dissolved, although he maintained his affluent practice, he seemed aimless for a time. He entered on a spiritual search to find meaning for his life. The new and more elevated purpose he had been looking for appeared in the form of inspired writings entitled *A Course in Miracles*. In them he found what he had been looking for, and it fit.

Not satisfied with merely finding what he needed for

himself, he set his task as serving others. First, as an affirmation of his faith, and much against my advice, he dropped his malpractice insurance, something that to most of us is an indispensable part of medical practice today. Then he gradually stopped charging those who came to him for help, believing that he should trust that his needs would be met if he dedicated himself to others.

He developed a program for children who had suffered catastrophic illnesses and accidents, such as cancer, leukemia, or head injuries. Based on the principles he had embraced, he helped them and their families to learn from these tragedies and to find peace.

From one program his influence has so spread that there are now centers in nearly every industrialized nation. He envisioned these children and others as emissaries of world peace. He created telephone networks of children, so they could share their own visions of their personal development and an enlightened world. He arranged exchanges among Arab and Israeli children, Americans and Soviets, Irish Protestants and Catholics.

I have seen him with these children, and it is quite remarkable. He does not tell them what to do, but supports them in expressing themselves. He seems to see in them not their weaknesses and disabilities, but what they can become—and they do. They discover strengths and love beyond what they believed they had; they shine like beacons to a troubled world.

That same vulnerable accessibility that I saw when I first met him has now found its full integrated expression in his loving work. He maintains the old belief that anything is possible, now manifested in the miraculous transformations in those he inspires.

And what of us? I must admit my skepticism about the path that he had chosen, and about the words, like "God" and "love," he used so freely, for I have often heard those words used to conceal more than they reveal. I doubted what he meant by them until I saw what he had done. And more and more I can recognize their reality.

Since I have been paralyzed, he has been there to help. And that has been both a support and a difficulty for me, because it no longer seems a relationship of equals, as it once was. Although I know his purpose certainly is not to do so, I feel diminished when I cannot do my part.

In friendship, being able to accept what is offered is just as important as giving and there must be room for both. When you are being cared for by another, you are in his hands and, no matter how well meaning he may be, inevitably he will do things in slightly different ways than you might. Who is in control may become an issue and, when it does, equality is denied; one person feels diminished, the other enhanced.

While giving help also serves a vital need for the one who gives, it can feel smothering for the one who receives. At those times you feel like the need that is being served is not yours at all. Sometimes I have felt that way. Even though I am physically dependent, it has often been difficult for me to allow people to help me. I must continually remind myself that accepting help graciously is as much a loving act as giving it.

Once I became annoyed by Jerry's efforts to help. I told him so. I said it was his presence I valued, and not what he could do for me. I meant it at the time, but now I realize it is not entirely true. He listened to my harsh words with utmost grace and sincerity—as he always does.

Another time I did have a major problem, but I didn't think it fair for me to ask for anyone's help. With that remarkable sensitivity I have come to know, Jerry intuitively perceived my need, and offered his help voluntarily. I was so overwhelmed by his generosity that I was moved to tears. Even after all these years, his accessibility still takes me by surprise.

Jerry can see the search for love behind each and every act, regardless of how cruel someone's behavior may appear to others. That deeply held belief surrounds him with his gentle benevolence. He believes that his love should be available equally to everyone, and that special relationships with selected others are too limiting. Although I understand that admirable ideal, the reality for me is that true friendships have not come easily and their number is never more than a few. They require time and commitment and my capacity for them is limited. I feel as if I am a special friend to Jerry and he to me and I selfishly want it to remain that way.

Jerry's love seems to know few bounds, and is not depleted by sharing it with everyone he meets; instead, it seems strengthened. I would like to be able to extend a friendship hand to all I meet, but clearly his capacity must be greater than mine.

He says that I am his brother, and I do believe that in some mysterious way I have always been. I am quite sure he loves me and maybe always did, but now I can take it in with fewer doubts and less criticism. And the strength of compassion he always had shines through more clearly now, no longer clouded by his own disquietude.

We live nearly five hundred miles apart, and Jerry is often traveling throughout the world in support of all that he believes. But we do remain in touch; we speak by telephone once or twice a week, and he visits me two or three times each year. And despite the demands upon his time, he has assured me that when I am in need, he will be here. I would like to do as much for him as he does for me, and he says that I do just that. Yet if I do, I do not see how, and, if it is true, it is another of the mysteries of the friendship bond.

NINE

Friendship Lost and Friendship Found: Ted

You can close your eyes to reality but not to memories.
—STANISLAW J. LEE

FOR THIRTY YEARS I was haunted by an incident of which I was so ashamed, I never mentioned it to a soul. It happened long ago, yet it festered in my mind like an unhealed wound. This is what happened, a tale of friendship and betrayal.

Ted was two years ahead of me at Stanford Medical School. We met because of tennis. Ted was not only a well-known tournament player, but a brilliant student too —at the very top of his class. I admired him greatly.

He had been invited to the Palm Springs Racquet Club to play exhibition matches with the club pro and the guests, and he asked me to join him. The club was owned by Charlie Farrell, an old movie star, and the guests were Hollywood's most famous celebrities. Ted and I would live at the club in luxury.

It was a remarkably welcome opportunity after the grind of both med school and working to support myself. We drove to Palm Springs in Ted's car, and had a memorable time enjoying life among the movie stars.

By the time we returned to school, we had become

good friends, and when time allowed, continued to play tennis, and even double-date occasionally. One night I had a heavy date for a party, and Ted generously loaned me his car. I parked the car in front of my girl's apartment, which was on a typical San Francisco hill, and went in to get her.

When we returned to the car, it was tightly wedged between two others. In trying to extricate Ted's car, I must have lightly touched the car downhill from me, although I felt no impact. Whatever happened, as I watched in helpless terror, the downhill car broke free and rolled backwards, crashing into a lamppost. Stunned, panicked, and confused, I got out to see what I could do.

No one seemed to be in sight. So I, still stunned, got back in the car and drove off, trying to escape. Although we went on to the party, I was so preoccupied with what had happened that my date was quickly going flat. Then Ted appeared at the party, looking for me. He was filled with well-controlled but justifiable anger.

It seemed that someone had taken down Ted's license number as we fled the scene. It was reported to the police, who in turn called Ted. He knew that I had his car, so the responsibility was mine. He confronted me.

Although I should have stayed and taken responsibility for my part, what made me so ashamed for many years was how I had responded to my friend's accusations. I was not forthcoming. Instead I acted like an accused child, insisting that I was innocent, and that the accident could not have been my fault. It was not the way a friend should respond to a friend.

But Ted was a friend and acted like one; although he was angry that I had not alerted him before, we went together to see the owner of the damaged car, and eventually the matter was left to insurance companies to settle.

The issue of betrayal that haunted me through the years had little to do with my guilt or innocence in the accident itself, for that was ambiguous at best. What haunted me was the way I treated a friend who had generously lent me his car—as an accusing enemy. He deserved better.

Ted soon graduated, moved away to pursue advanced medical training in Cincinnati, and we lost touch. However, I kept my guilty secret within me, and watched it grow. When I first became disabled and looked for reasons to explain why this illness had befallen me, my betrayal of his friendship came to mind as an explanation, however twisted that may seem now.

I had no word from Ted for over thirty years, although I still thought about those events. One day, quite to my surprise, I received a telephone call from him. Much had happened in his life, and certainly in mine. The last time we had met was probably on the tennis court.

Ted had become a specialist in internal medicine, and practiced brilliantly for a time. Then he became fascinated by the effect the mind had on illnesses. To further this interest he trained more, and became a psychiatrist.

Now, in addition to his busy practice, he was director of education at a hospital near San Francisco.

Having read a professional paper I had written, he invited me to speak to the hospital staff. His special interest was mind-body relationships, something of both personal and professional concern to me.

My immediate thought was that at long last this was an opportunity for me to rectify what had remained unhealed. However, I was still puzzled about why he had called me, considering our last encounter. Why would he call on me at all? I was afraid of what he might think of me if I told the truth of those long-ago events. Nevertheless, I wanted to get it over with, so I told him that I would like to meet alone with him while I was there. He agreed, and we planned to have lunch together before my talk.

He thoughtfully selected a quiet grill where we could talk. Although the food was superb, my attention was divided, for I was quite preoccupied with what would happen. After he finished eating, I carefully approached the subject.

He seemed puzzled at first, and could not even recall the events. He did not remember loaning me his car, and nothing of my involvement in an accident. My big sin, my fearful confession, and all my fears were quickly going flat. I pressed on with more and more details of my shame and betrayal, until at last he showed a flicker of interest. But, alas, it was only in how I remembered him reacting.

Nevertheless, I had purged myself of something that

had bothered me for more than half my life. Although he did not need to say the words, he had forgiven me; in fact, despite my protestations, he did not see that there was very much that needed to be forgiven. I now felt relieved of my burden.

So what am I to make of all of this, and what does it have to do with friendship? Thinking of it now in the light of day and exposed to the healing rays of sunshine, my big betrayal seems quite trivial—nothing more than could have been expected from me as a teenager.

Still, it compromised who and what I thought I was; it had come to symbolize all the times when I did not, would not behave as I believed I should, and when my integrity had failed. And what is more important than to be true to oneself?

To remind me of that, I keep an old-fashioned ashtray in the corner of my office. In college I had stolen it from a rival fraternity, considered a great coup, and popularly interpreted at the school as showing daring and courage. Today it serves a purpose similar to my failed integrity with Ted.

I do not blame myself too much for the ashtray; taking it was only doing what was considered collegiate at the time. Yet that is important, because although it may have seemed all right at the time, it is not now. One can only live with what is known at the time, and while that may attenuate culpability a bit, it does not, in the long run, limit responsibility or absolve a person from making amends.

I did try to return the ashtray, but there was no one to receive it. The house was gone, the organization disbanded. To have simply gotten rid of it would have served only to make me feel better. So instead, I keep it around as a just reminder—that nearly every choice has ethical consequences, and should be made with as much care as one can muster.

My experiences with Ted and the problematic ashtray also serve as reminders that unhealed wounds should not be allowed to fester. When you hide things, as I did, they begin to seem worse and worse, like a carbuncle growing on the soul. Since no fresh light or air is allowed in to purify, the contamination only grows.

Confession and absolution relieve the soul, but the emphasis should be on the healing and the restoration of fractured relationships. Modest goals perhaps, but their value is unmistakable.

And that is where friendship must come in: With a friend who's true, you must be true; if not, you're not allowing him the full privileges of friendship. You will treat a friend with as much integrity as you treat yourself.

My editor Casey once said she thought that loyalty distinguishes a friend from just anybody. I can see the wisdom of that, because my secret betrayal of Ted kept me from continuing our friendship for thirty years—not because of anything he did or did not do, but because my lack of candor—real or imagined—caused me to avoid him.

Since we had our meeting, good faith has been restored, and we are friends again, even better than before. Although we live half a state apart, we speak often on the telephone, and whenever Ted comes south I have the pleasure of his visit. As I have come to know Ted and his artist wife Peggy, I have discovered much to admire.

Believing strongly that they wished to contribute more to life than they had done, in recent years they have looked abroad. Although Ted has been helping others as a doctor, and he and Peggy have raised a fine family, they became concerned about Third World refugees. They volunteered to go to Africa to see what they might do to help the desperate populations in Ethiopia and Sudan.

They surveyed the needs and established health-care programs and clinics. On their regular visits to refugee camps they continue to see that the facilities function well and are adequately staffed. Since hunger and refugees go hand in hand, Ted and Peggy have developed expertise in food needs; they consult and collaborate on these matters, and involve other private and governmental agencies.

A spectacular photograph of the Taj Mahal, taken by Peggy, hangs in our living room. In addition to the pleasure the picture brings to the viewer, it also serves as an important reminder: that all is rarely lost, that a fractured bond of hope and friendship can be restored through truth and openness from you, and from a friend.

TEN

Serendipity: A Friend Appears in Time of Need

A friend cannot be known in prosperity . . .
—Ecclesiasticus

IN THE WESTERN WORLD, people tend to think of themselves as individuals first, last, and always, like separate objects in time and space. However, if one can keep an open mind, evidence also appears to demonstrate that we are joined together as one—though perhaps on different planes of awareness.

Sometimes when there seems no way out of a situation, someone appears, seemingly out of nowhere, to help in astonishing ways. That is when I am aware of how I am connected with others, even if I don't know quite how. The encounter may be brief, but includes acts of such loving generosity that they can never be forgotten. They must be called acts of friendship, yet it must be friendship without past kinship or personal history.

Where do the people who do these remarkable things come from? How does it happen that they are available at the very time you need them? The thing that amazes me is that they are not usually full-time saints at all, but ordinary human beings with every conceivable emotion and desire. It seems that no matter how much we may try to deny it, there is some of Mother Teresa in us all—and probably some of Hitler, too.

Consider this example. A stranger walks by a house that bursts into flame. He makes a choice. Does he wait around to loot the place? Does he rush away to save himself? Or does he see the house as if it were his own and stay to put the fire out? Does he rush in to rescue a helpless child? However he reacts, it is likely to be without forethought. Is there a hand that guides him in his choice?

When I first got sick with polio, I hovered between life and death for many weeks. Although I was completely paralyzed and unable to speak or breathe on my own, I found such a friend—or perhaps he found me.

It was during the Korean War, and I had been recalled into the navy. Since I got sick shortly after reporting to duty, I was a patient in a navy hospital. There were many different doctors, nurses, and corpsmen assigned to care for me. In addition there were, from time to time, doctors I had known who were temporarily stationed there awaiting overseas duty. They all did their jobs, and some came for friendly visits. But my needs were greater than could be fulfilled by assignment or occasional visits.

The hospital's power frequently went out and, without electricity, my iron lung would stop working, and I would stop breathing. My beard, which always kept growing, would interfere with the life-sustaining collar seal on the machine. There was no one assigned to manually pump the iron lung, and no barber to cut my beard. That is when a new friend magically appeared.

He was a full commander (impressive, since I was a lowly lieutenant junior grade), a urologist who had been a chief of service at the hospital where I interned. He had been recalled to duty at the same time I was. And, in keeping with the navy's capacity to foul things up, he had been assigned to be an orthopedist. Since he was not trained in orthopedics, he was given no duties.

He heard about me through mutual friends, and came to make a friendly visit. Observing my growth of beard, he returned with a razor and shaved it off. That night the power went off, and I stopped breathing. Suddenly he appeared, well before anyone else, and began hand-pumping the iron lung. For some weeks thereafter, whenever the power went out, he was there to pump and see if anyone else had come. He kept me alive through the most acute part of my hospitalization.

Then one day they shipped him out, and I never saw him again. Years later, when I was able, I searched for him and discovered he lived and worked in Texas. I wrote to thank him for what he had done. He seemed hardly to remember these events that were so vivid to me. I kept in touch for several years after, but clearly to him it was a minor event, so eventually we lost contact.

A minor event of little consequence for him; a lifesaving act of love for me. How little we know of each other! We are all imprisoned by being able to view the world from only one perspective. Yet even while others may have limited awareness of what our view may be, they still can have profound effects on us and we on them.

After I was transferred to a civilian rehabilitation hospital, another such event occurred. I had been in bed for two years, because I could sit erect in a wheelchair for only about five minutes a day. I needed a wheelchair that would easily allow adjustment of my body's position, from sitting up to lying down without returning to bed. That was very expensive and I had no means to pay for it. My last job was as an intern, at ten dollars per month. I was just lucky that most of my hospitalization was covered by the March of Dimes Foundation.

The only other person in the hospital as severely affected as me was Helen, whom I had never seen, since neither of us was mobile. But I got to know about her through Jack, her husband. In his visits to her, which were once or twice each day, he would often stop to chat with me too.

Although I never said a word about my wheelchair need, Jack and Helen learned of it. And one day, the very model that I needed appeared at my bedside as a gift from them. I was deeply touched by their generosity, but they never seemed to want any credit for what they had done and neither of them ever mentioned it or expected anything in return. We continued as good friends and I have remained profoundly grateful to them.

After we left the hospital, Helen and I were especially close through the years, for we had so much to share. She went back to school in spite of her extreme disability, became a clinical social worker and practiced for a while. She was a remarkable woman and, as she had done with mine, she touched many other lives very deeply. A few years ago, to my sorrow, she passed away; my loss and grief were, of course, far less momentous than Jack's. However, our common loss brought us closer than before.

Jack and I speak by phone nearly every day, and those conversations have become an important evening ritual. We sometimes bet small amounts on sports, and occasionally play backgammon. We also have some more serious interests in common like health-care services and people who have disabilities. Yet we are remarkably different in many ways.

As a mutual friend once said of Jack, "Some people seem born to be kings." On one's first glimpse of him the reason is apparent, for he is very tall with regal bearing. He moves and acts with courtly manners and his self-assurance is befitting of royalty. He was the youngest naval officer to command a ship in World War II, and in his life after the war he has maintained command in corporate and philanthropic activities.

He is a person who understands the uses of power, and consequently uses it wisely and well. When Jack speaks, people listen carefully and usually comply. His confidence and directness of approach must be the keys, I think. His purposes are always designed to help and his authority is most often felt in support of various hospitals, universities, and other special causes. But he is at his best when the cause is helping someone else.

A Friend Appears in Time of Need 109

When he entertains his friends, each person feels cared for abundantly. His goal is the pleasure of his friends. There are so many qualities and actions for which I admire him, and many were begun with Helen at his side. I am still moved when I recall their generosity to me, many years ago. And when I think of their timely friendship, then and now, I feel humble gratitude.

When someone appears out of nowhere to help another in need, is it just dumb luck, a matter of coincidence? Or is it guided in some mysterious way? The same question comes to mind when something terrible occurs as well—a "drive-by" murder of an innocent bystander, or, for that matter, the apparent random attack by a polio virus.

Maybe a partial answer is that there are always saviors nearby, and instruments of harm as well. But because our capacity to see and comprehend is so narrow and necessarily skewed, we can see only what we expect. When we expect to be rescued, a rescuer appears. When we expect to be hurt, evil appears. I sometimes wonder if there is much of anything in the world out there, or if all we see is from inside.

When I was director of an education and research center in the 1960s, I hired work-study students from the university for various part-time jobs. They often became quite attached to Rita and myself, and we to them. Bob, a big gregarious fellow, became especially involved, and continued to stay in touch long after he left the center and the university. Bob always willingly offered to help with my personal care when I needed him—something he did with sensitivity and skill.

Sometimes a year or two went by without a word from him, then he would appear and we would see a lot of him for several weeks. Bob was very bright, energetic, and witty, with a remarkable capacity for both self-indulgence and generosity. Within ten years he had amassed a fortune, complete with homes in Hawaii, Palm Springs, and San Francisco. He had a fleet of luxury cars, and kept a sixty-foot yacht fully manned for his occasional use.

Once, I was having a lot of breathing problems and hospitalization was necessary, but I refused to go. Hospitals are inherently dangerous places, and even more unpredictably hazardous if you are paralyzed and helpless. They are efficient places for the staff, because there is a routine for everything. Unfortunately, many of the routines do not fit me. For example, the routine for lifting patients depends on a patient having stable hips and shoulders, but mine are not. The nursing staff insist on doing things their way, consistent with their union contract.

I had not seen Bob in a long time, when he suddenly called I mentioned my problem about breathing and the hospital. To my astonishment he said, "Don't worry, I'll take a week off and take care of you there." And indeed he did. He charmed the hospital staff into letting him sleep on the ward in the bed next to mine. He was there and ready to help twenty-four hours a day, and responsively did all of my personal care.

Not only did he take superb care of me, but he helped many of the other patients on the understaffed ward as well. He saved the life of at least one patient by giving artificial respiration. He helped everyone. When we left, I had worked out a plan to alleviate my respiratory problem, and was none the less for wear, all thanks to Bob.

Such selfless acts of love and friendship must affect the world well beyond those in whose memory they consciously remain. Bob freely took a week out of his multimillion-dollar deal-making life to help a friend in the most elemental way—he brushed my teeth, took me to the bathroom, whatever I needed. It was a far cry from his world of high finance, helping me with my most fundamental primitive needs.

But Bob either always knew or perhaps later discovered that money and material things had limited use for him. Today, after two failed marriages, the money and possessions are almost all gone, and he says he is much happier. Now he lives a very simple life by himself in a tiny house.

Although I have often spoken to him of his kindness, he has never mentioned it, nor does he seem to regard it as anything special. But it certainly is to me. Could it be that it *was* no sacrifice for him, as I assumed, and it was just as right for him as it was for me?

Perhaps that is one of the vital characteristics of friendship, that there is no sense of sacrifice in helping a friend, and there is no sense of debt. Nobody owes anybody anything; you do something for a friend without encumbrance and without expectation. Your friend's fate is like your own, so that responding is as natural as taking care of yourself.

To the commander, Jack and Helen, and Bob, my needs were apparent and they responded—that's all. The help seemed to take very little effort for them, but had a monumental effect on me, which I shall never forget.

How often do we give up opportunities to help another? A chance for real immortality, the only kind that counts, and we pass it up. These are avenues by which we can reach a rock star's brief celebrity. But we are wary, too. We often think, "Does this person really need my help, or is it just a scam?"

We hate to be pushovers and would feel ashamed if someone took us in. It would remind us of the deep-seated childhood shame we felt when we were small and weak and at the mercy of others. This may provide good reason for copping out, and there are, unfortunately, many people who seek unfair advantage. But should childhood shame be sufficient justification for avoiding an opportunity to dwell in the hearts of others for what may be eternity?

And eternity is precisely what is at stake, for that is where we all will dwell when this transitory moment is over. I do not in any way diminish the importance of this moment and the form in which I live—it is all that I really do know today. But to live as if it were all that counted forever would be to live as a blind and selfish fool. I must strive to make the responsibilities that I feel within this space and time consistent with the universe and my fate within it, too.

ELEVEN

Teacher, Collaborator, Friend: Fritz

A friend hears the song in my heart and sings it to me
when my memory fails.
                              —*Pioneer Girls Leaders' Handbook*

FOR A DECADE I felt my disability was hopeless. I could "like it or lump it," as we used to say in elementary school. Well, I certainly did not like it, and I could never figure out what "lump it" meant. What I did was accept it grudgingly, and try to make the best of it.

From the standpoint of the outer world, I was doing pretty well, or, at least, as well as could be expected, considering that I was paralyzed from the neck down. I had gone back to work, was self-supporting, had a lovely wife, and I had become the director of a training program for psychiatrists.

So what did I have to complain about? Nothing, I thought! I was doing as well as possible, considering how disabled I was. And I did not complain aloud, for I was well aware that I could just as easily be on welfare and not have the things I did have. I knew the fate of some of my disabled friends, just as capable as I was, who never made it out of an institutional setting. I was lucky.

So I kept my mouth shut, did my work, lived as best I

could, and that was that! But although I felt I had no justification for complaint, I was miserable. I was deprived of the physical pleasures that had been my raison d'etre and, thus I was not living the way I wanted. Action, sports, speed, were what I desired—but, instead, I was trapped in an alien body that belonged to some cripple I did not know or care much about. This is not who I really am, I thought. But all I could do was either "like it or lump it."

I went into analysis, and learned quite a bit more about myself. I liked the process, and was fond of the two analysts with whom I worked over those several years. They were decent, intelligent, and well-meaning, but I did not feel any better about myself. The experience further convinced me that mine was a bitter reality that I must grudgingly accept. I did not yet understand that there are always multiple realities from which to choose.

Part of the problem was that being paralyzed was such a good rationalization for feeling miserable that people, no matter what their profession, could see no way out, and could only commiserate. I desperately wanted something better, but could not see how to go about it. Neither could the people whom I had hired to help me; they were incapacitated by my disability, just as I was.

I had really abandoned hope of feeling any better about my life. I thought that by becoming a more competent psychiatrist I would be more highly regarded by others, which might make me feel better about myself. My goal was off the mark, but in its pursuit I reached another place.

I had become training director fresh out of my own training, so I still had much to learn. In designing the program I planned projects that would foster not only the education of the residents, but my own as well. The format I used brought the world's acknowledged experts in psychiatry and related fields to stay at the hospital to work and to teach for brief times—from a day or two to several weeks. In that process I met many of the best-known people in the field.

Rita and I lived in a home on the hospital grounds and I would invite these men and women to stay with us, so that I not only participated in their daytime teaching activities, but I also had them to myself in the evenings. I did my best to learn all I could. Although it was not conscious, I think I was secretly seeking my own salvation.

Whenever possible I would try to have some therapy time with them for myself, ostensibly to expand my knowledge and skills from their different perspectives. It was an amazing experience, which sometimes confirmed their reputations, and sometimes not at all. I remember one famous analyst, whose writings I had loved, appeared as an utter fraud in actual practice. But that was unusual.

I wanted only the best teachers, to enhance the prestige of the program and support the elitist position to which I aspired. I had no interest in unrecognized innovators. So, when Fritz Perls, whom I had never heard of, called to say that he wanted to teach in the program, I gave him a cold reception. Then I heard from another training director that he had been the most outstanding teacher my colleague ever had, so I called him back.

His first words to me when we met were, "What happened to you?" He said them with such childlike innocence and wonder that I did not take offense. He simply seemed interested in the obvious, which was a great contrast to the usual reactions. Most people do not know how to react to someone who is severely disabled, so they awkwardly blurt out something inappropriate, express their own discomfort, or just ignore the whole thing. Then I have to try to reassure them or join in the stilted avoidance. To me, his refreshingly candid reaction showed nothing more than honest interest. It was a relief.

Fritz Perls was a maverick, a Berlin-trained psychoanalyst who rebelled against those teachers whose authority he admired. He looked a little down at the heels, like an elderly hippie in a rumpled suit. In addition to his Freudian perspective, he had also worked in Frankfurt am Main amidst the beginnings of gestalt psychology, and out of that found his own ground. He integrated fragments of knowledge and experience without remembering their sources. Although he never mentioned it, and I knew him for months before I discovered it, he called his system Gestalt Therapy. But his real power was in his capacity to make contact immediately with the essence of people and their situations.

One of the favorite devices used by resident doctors to

test their teachers is to present them with the most extreme and refractory cases. And in a large psychiatric hospital, some cases are impossibly bizarre, and the patients have failed to respond to every possible intervention. Fritz, as he insisted everyone call him, was challenged with several of these therapeutically imponderable cases with remarkable results.

He quickly reached them where they were at their best, so that during the interviews with him, they were not at all as we had known them before. All of their strange behavior and eerie speech patterns seemed clearly comprehensible for the first time. He had made contact with their strengths.

And that is exactly what he did with me as well. Although he would not have used these words, he showed me that I was the architect of how I saw my world, and not its helpless victim. I felt understood and empowered by him. He listened carefully, and using my own words with a slight characterization, showed me what I had said. This made my words stand out, so even I could see that I had choices I had not seen before.

He was a free man who showed me the basis of his freedom—that he lived here and now, in the only moment where one is not entrapped by one's own beliefs and by patterns from the past. He showed me that when I was firmly in this moment and this place, the options grew. I learned how I could live using the energy that exists in the here and now, although I also learned that I had a major role in the creation of the future that I wanted. All of this may seem quite obvious to you, as intellectually it did to me, but to know it in my heart and to be able to use it was new to me.

Our relationship was different from the impersonal ones I had known before when I was in analysis. With Fritz, everything was entirely personal, and there was no way to avoid what was real. I saw him under many different circumstances, and he was always the same person. Since he was living in our house, I saw him at dinner, at work, on awakening, and when retiring. He loved all of life equally—each person was unique and yet the same for him. He lived as he believed.

After dinner, we would sit and talk. I ostensibly was trying to learn how he worked and thought. In retrospect, I realized that in addition to wanting to improve my work, I was looking to see if there was hope for me in what he knew and did. He offered the choice to me to talk or use him as a therapist. I protested that the structure of our relationship was inconsistent with good therapy, which generally thrives on having an objective therapist. He patiently considered each of my concerns with me.

I had quite a catalog of specific misgivings about what he was doing, and a lot about this unconventional maverick himself. I was both conventional and cautious. However, as soon as I began to work with him, I could see for the first time that there were other ways to view my disability than as a dreadful curse.

I did not intend to learn so much from him. But he

had no fear of my fragility, so neither, then, did I. I would ask him a question from my intellect, often designed to enhance my weakened belief in myself. He would counter with disarming gentle directness, asking whether I wanted only to talk about it, or to *do* something to change my misery.

He was paid by the hospital for his teaching activities. He did not seem to care whether I paid for my individual time or not. I did, because I thought structure was required, but it mattered not to him. I grieved for my lost physical abilities, I got angry at him for all sorts of things. And eventually I loved him too (emotions I hadn't allowed in previous analysis and therapy.)

This unconventional arrangement was ideal for my physical limitations, for it required no travel, an arduous task for me at best. And he was consistent, caring, direct —sometimes uncomfortably so. When he was away, he wrote interesting letters to me about his travels (and they were many).

Initially, he spent one week at the hospital. He was so impressive in his demonstrations with patients that we asked him to return whenever possible. After that he returned every other week for several years. In a week's time I would get four to five individual hours with him, and two or three in groups he led with residents and staff. He gradually involved me as co-leader, and eventually, although I was reluctant, I led groups on my own. In addition, he demonstrated his work with selected patients, so I had a broad experience with him.

He was in his late sixties, and confidently knew his ground. He was not so different from other fine therapists and analysts, except on the level of his personal integration. This consistency had its problems in other areas of his life, and made him a less than faithful spouse and an inconsistent parent. But as a therapist, he was a genius.

Everyone Fritz encountered, and many people he had not met, held strong opinions about him that ranged from love to hate. His influence was personal, and those who knew him or at least knew others who had been deeply touched by him were almost always affected positively. His reputation suffered from some who simply read his written works or who adopted only some superficial gesture of his, and then assumed that was all there was.

Many people today who do not recognize the power of what he did and said dismiss him lightly. There are many who faithfully do represent his work, although sometimes their competence is glibly denied as nothing more than "unresolved positive transference," or worse. However, his critics' loss is theirs. His influence has been far wider than is sometimes credited.

His legacy has been limited by several things: his unconventional life-style, his disrespect for authority, and, most of all, one of his strongly held beliefs. He sought to foster and support individual freedom and choice in all he encountered, so the allegiance of those he trained was to themselves and far exceeded any loyalty to him.

Strong individualists do not create good followers and he insisted on autonomy. As a result, many who learned from him failed to credit him, and instead have developed their own schemes and their own followers; many who were dependent on affiliations have returned to the groups from which they came. But even they are not the same, for they have grown.

Other schools of psychotherapy have gradually adopted and assimilated his views, but rarely credited him as the source. He influenced the evolution of the whole field, even though his name is sometimes lost. And since he believed that fact—not the name—is important, perhaps he would be pleased. Anyhow, it is a just irony that a man who rarely recalled the source of what he had learned should now be treated just the same.

Although he basked in the adulation of those he met, he was ambivalent about any who followed in his name. So today, although there are Gestalt Therapy Institutes in many places around the world where his work and views flourish, they received little or no support from him. He lived as he believed, in this elusive moment as if it were forever.

He died in his late seventies following surgery. His final spoken words were to a nurse and exemplified his belief in individual autonomy. She had told him to get back in bed. From the convictions of a lifetime, he firmly answered: "Don't tell me what to do." Then he died.

His last words to me came after his death. Curiously, I read them in his autobiography, *In and Out of the Garbage Pail,* a book filled with his own aberrant art and poetry. After a brief introduction about a paper I had written on change, he wrote:

"I have known Arnie for so many years. Hello, Arnie. It's good to be with you, if only in fantasy. I know we love each other, and yet we are hardly ever free from self-consciousness when we meet. You look so fragile in your [wheel] chair. I never asked you how it feels not to be able to stretch your arms freely when you want to embrace somebody. What courage to come to terms with life after being deeply involved with sports and then being stricken with infantile paralysis, hardly managing to survive.

"How are you doing in your training center? How is Rita? I want to tell you what an excellent paper you wrote. So few people understand the paradox of change."

So, since fantasy is also possible for me:

Hello, Fritz. I hope you have found some peace, wherever you may be. Rita is fine, even though she has had some rough times of her own with health. Thank you, Fritz, for all you did for me. You were a friend who came into my life at just the right time. I learned so much from you. Although you congratulate me on my change paper, I could not have conceived it except as a result of my work with you. You helped me to make new sense of my disability. You helped me to trust in what may come, and to understand that no matter what occurs, I always will have some choices open to me.

Fritz Perls is remembered today as a guru or god by some; others consider him the devil incarnate. He was one of the most influential figures of the sixties and an architect of the human potential movement. Certainly he has had a major impact on the directions of all psychotherapy practice.

To me he was a friend—always honest, kind, and generous. The limitations in our friendship were dictated by me. Certainly that was true for my insistence on "structure" when I began to work with him. I rarely tested the limits of his friendship, but when I did, I was never denied. When Rita and I visited at his home in Big Sur, he offered us his only bed and bedroom. When I asked him for help with my physical care, he was more than willing. (I asked only rarely.)

Everyone has some god and devil within, but I could never find his evil part. He was accused of many bad things, and often I confronted him when I heard a specific rumor. Sometimes they were based on distortions of his work by followers, and sometimes from offense taken by some at his intuitiveness and honesty. I never saw him do anything with malice. I was never able to substantiate any claim that he was unethical, although some who claimed him as guru were. The only time I saw him at his worst was when he was visited by Eric Berne, another famed innovator. They both behaved like competitive children, trying to establish dominance.

He was not only my therapist, he was my first spiritual

guide (although he would never have used those words). He sought the love and truth and beauty that lay beneath all that was mundane or seamy. Once when Rita and I returned from a trip to Yosemite, I told him about the awesome Grizzly Giant Sequoia redwood tree. I told him how on first viewing it I felt transformed by its majesty. It dwarfed all of the surrounding trees, and it appeared to me that they were kneeling there, while worshipping its stately nobility. Although it was late at night when I told him this, and he was old and tired, he arose and left immediately to drive hundreds of miles to see for himself.

He had seen the horrors of World War I in trenches as a young German doctor, and his entire family was killed in the Holocaust. His obsession became finding the truth and beauty in the world. In his work with patients, his greatest joy was when he released love entrapped by hate and fear. He had faith that when the negative was purged, the basic good of man emerged.

There is a time in middle life when it becomes necessary to find a means of integrating who you were when growing up with who you really want to be. Most of us need a guide to help us find our way, a teacher who has traveled that road before. Fritz was mine, and in the process opened me to finding others too. He was loving without being possessive, and he was wise in the ways I needed him to be.

This is a description of a dear friend as I knew him, so he may well have been different with others in his life. I cannot say. I do realize more and more that, with a friend, it is never just you and him or her, for two are together as one. Reactions are not just those of separate individuals, so much as what you have become together. And genuine friendship brings out the best of both of you to share.

TWELVE

Girl Friends

You don't have to suffer to be a poet. Adolescence is enough suffering for anyone. —JOHN CIARDI

WHEN YOU GROW UP without sisters, you develop distorted views about girls. That's what happened to me. Our small family consisted only of my mother and father and my brother and me, making my mother the only feminine influence there, and she always tended to subordinate herself to supporting the rest of us. There were not even any girls my age in the neighborhood, so they remained an arcane mystery.

I knew how to relate to "mothers," but not to female peers. So, when I started school and had my first encounters with them, I was puzzled, to say the least. Enigmatic creatures, indeed, like boys in so many ways, but so different in others. And, of course, they stimulated those unfamiliar and nameless stirrings inside me. I just had no idea how to act around them.

However, it was no big problem in grade school because the boys seemed to unite against the girls. Anyone who spent time with girls was considered a traitor and branded a sissy. It's a lot different now—kids are much more open, and grade-schoolers even date and sometimes even experiment with sex.

We boys played sports, got dirty, had fights, and built tree houses. I do not know what the girls did, nor did I even care very much. We met them in class, where we did our best to taunt or ignore them because they liked school, were smarter, got better grades, were always clean, and seemed to enjoy all the things we hated. All girls were sissies except for an occasional tomboy, and we were not sure what to make of them.

Strange indeed, that boys who liked girls were considered "sissies" instead of heterosexual, and girls who liked boys were "tomboys" instead of heterosexual. In the grade school battle of the sexes there were no noncombatants or liaisons. You either had to be "with 'em or against 'em, one of us or one of them."

But it was all a misleading bluff! Secretly we all harbored thoughts of love—although we did not know what it was, or even where to begin. Dorothea was my girl-friend—after all, I thought, she showed me clearly how she felt when she smiled at me. Several times I caught her looking at me—or was it she who caught me looking at her? We never spoke, and the only thing I ever remember exchanging were furtive glances.

Occasionally we boys *did* talk about girls, and we each had our favorites. When Billy told me that Lois, the smartest girl in our class, "stank" and was "stupid," I knew something did not fit, but I did not recognize these as professions of love for her. And there were intimate moments with our best friends, when we saw no contradiction between admitting that "so-and-so is my girl" and our conviction that we hated all girls.

By the time I reached puberty, and with it junior high school, I was thoroughly confused, and had no good way of relating with girls. So I ignored them, as I had learned to do in grade school, yet I also spent enormous amounts of time thinking about them. Much of the time I was a lot like my big Chesapeake Bay retriever Barney, who, when neighborhood female dogs are in heat, has no outlet to express himself; he wanders around aimlessly, not knowing what to do. In my case, if it were not for sports, I probably would have gone quite mad.

Moreover, I was now alone in my misery. All the other guys who had sisters or had otherwise grown up with girls were now dating, instead of just thinking about it. They were also talking openly about women, but I had nothing acceptable to discuss. This left me not only isolated from girls, but somewhat distanced from the boys as well.

Fortunately, basketball, football, track, and other sports allowed me to express my energies, and I did with all-out commitment. I was still "one of the guys," and admired by the girls in athletics; no wonder I threw myself into them with so much enthusiasm.

High school was much the same, and my sense of isolation grew. Sports remained my only salvation. Girls would sometimes be quite forward about their interest in me. When they would want to get together, I would think of some subterfuge to avoid it. It was really crazy: Although I thought about them constantly, when opportunities appeared, I would run.

I did have a few dates, but I was so awkward they were usually disasters. The first time I actually asked a girl for a date was when my friend Hal had four tickets to a play and wanted to double-date. In a counterphobic impulse, I decided to ask Dorothy, one of the prettiest and most popular girls in school.

She worked at Woolworth's on Saturdays, so I thought I would be very casual about the whole thing and act as if I had just run into her there. I spotted her behind a counter and nonchalantly wandered over, being careful not to seem to notice her, and began examining the merchandise.

Then, in panic, I realized I was inspecting needles and thread. (My God, I thought, why does it have to be needles and thread, why not baseballs or even flashlights?). I was red-faced, mortified, considering the relative merits of white, black, brown, and other colors of thread, exposed in front of the one person I so wanted to impress!

Then I discovered I could not look up at her. My head was stuck! I tried and tried, but could not look up beyond the threads. I did not know whether to run or stay; I was caught and fully unmasked. Then, still not looking at her, to my surprise I heard myself saying: "You wanna go out next Saturday night?" I think I heard someone, I guess it was Dorothy, answer something like, "I've already got a date." But by then I found myself out on the street.

Another embarrassing time was with Barbara, an equally popular and sophisticated girl whom I was mad about. I asked her to the DeMolay open dance on a Friday night, an act of blind courage, since I could barely dance at the time. Not wanting to display my awkwardness on the dance floor, I was just standing around and saying hardly anything to her. When, quite naturally, other boys would ask her to dance, she did, and the more she seemed to enjoy herself, the more unhappy I became.

Her ease and popularity intensified my feelings of being an outcast—I suppose I must have wanted her to stand around and be miserable with me. Outrage is the cover for humiliation—the last recourse of the powerless. Of course, recognizing that it was irrational, I did not wish to expose myself further, so I just pouted—not terribly effective punishment for someone as comfortable with people as Barbara was—she just ignored it.

By now you must be getting the idea. To round out the picture, I must say my awkwardness was evidently not so apparent to others, who tell me I seemed quite normal. If so, I kept an awful lot hidden, and I'll bet Dorothy and Barbara were not fooled.

Going to college and then into the navy provided new starts for me, and I began dating with a vengeance. I discovered a convenient and familiar model for relating to girls my own age—competitive sports. I had a lot of company with that model, for often it was impossible among my athletic friends to recognize the differences in goals between a football game and a date.

We wanted to win. You could win by "scoring." To score you had to have the right moves and plays. The right strategy was also necessary. The assumption was that boys were always on the offense, trying to score, and girls were always on the defense, trying to protect home base. That there might be some mutual basis for interest came as a real eye-opener when it finally dawned on me.

As dehumanizing as that may sound, I learned much. At first winning was getting a girl into bed, but to do that I had to learn how to talk with and interest them. Besides, after enough shallow victories, I began to want something more substantial. I consciously tried to make platonic friends with women, and I often did. However, to do so meant a vigilant suppression of sexual feelings struggling for expression.

In my early twenties I had become an itinerant doctor/tennis player. I worked in San Francisco, and then New Orleans, and every chance I got I was off to a tournament. With my travels I met many people, and I was beginning to be more sophisticated about both men and women.

So, in spite of myself and the competitive sports model, I began to learn a little about the world of the other sex beyond the stereotypes I held. I was a slow learner, however. Women first became human to me when I concluded, "Oh, I see; they are just like men, only different." As limiting as that was, it was a step in the right direction, but a long way from a real understanding.

All of this time I was behaving conventionally, and probably looked quite ordinary. I liked women, I sometimes loved them, I dated a lot, I went steady, I was kind and usually considerate. I was also very naive, and did not understand.

Then, when I became disabled, I began to integrate more of what I had learned. That may seem a high price to pay for the privilege of relating to women, but—as I have since learned—if you remain open, there usually is an up side to every down.

Since I could not move at all, I became an observer—the only thing I could do well—and in hospitals, most of the people you meet in patient care are women. For the first time I began to see them as they really were—not in the context of some preformed category.

My education took a quantum leap when I met Rita, who later was to become my wife of what is now nearly forty years. She was lovely and sexy, but so much more to me. We became not only lovers, but best friends. She was lover, friend, helpmate, and, in what seemed a near miracle, the sister I never had. In fact, people often thought we were brother and sister.

At first I thought we were alike, and we are in many ways, but each day we live together, I see how different we are also. Is that not the very essence of relating, being connected to another—to care for him or her as you do yourself, while respecting and acknowledging the differences?

I traveled a tortuous path before I learned how to be a friend to women. I am not proud of the route, but I am pleased with the outcome. Today, I am happy to report, I have a number of good friends who are women—proving that there is life after sports.

I do not understand women, for they are not to be understood—any more than men are. But I do see more and more in individual women to appreciate. Yes, women are different from men, and they are also different from other women. There is still a latent sexual element in all men/women relationships for me; however, it is not usually manifest all the time. And just as they are free to choose if it ever will be, so am I.

THIRTEEN

Derivative Friends

We cannot tell the precise moment when friendship is formed. As in filling a vessel drop by drop, there is at last a drop which makes it run over; so in a series of kindnesses there is at last one which makes the heart run over.
—JAMES BOSWELL

THE TERM "fair-weather friend" is an oxymoron, for if a person is only a friend when times are good, he is no friend at all. Rock and movie stars must, I imagine, be wary of such people, but it has not been a concern for me. Initially what attracts a person to a potential friend may be obscure, and the relationship will likely be tenuous at first. However, once it has been established, mutual support usually begins to feel quite natural. And since friends are freely chosen from all the acquaintances we make, we must be just as free to change our minds about who will continue to be friends.

When two people get a divorce, much attention is paid to who will get the custody of the children. And it is just as important with their friends: Who will get their custody? Although usually not a part of the settlement, it is a critical time when both the former wife and husband need all the support they can get. And in spite of all efforts to keep both as friends, a split is rarely avoided. Conflict and dissolution sadly seem the rule, and acrimony instead of harmony.

It is only natural to see the same perspective as a friend, and want to take his part. In conflict between two friends, who once were one, it is hard on everyone if a third friend is forced to choose between them. One of the former partners will usually feel hurt and abandoned if the other gets some sympathy from their mutual friends. And the friends feel so torn that they often choose one over the other, if only just to simplify and avoid being caught in the conflict.

But a friend is still a friend, and worthy of whatever difficulties may arise. After wrenching divorces where my efforts to help both partners drew me unwittingly into the conflict, I have made a rule for myself. I tell friends getting a divorce, at the outset, that I do not want to be forced to abandon either, and that I want to continue to be a friend with each, so I will not take sides or talk of one to the other. I have found it helps to some extent, but still I must be vigilant to avoid being seen as aligned with one against the other.

A friend is a friend is a friend! Whatever the source of the friendship, and whatever strains emerge to test the relationship, it is worth every effort to try to save it. To casually exchange one friendship for another is to declare that none of them is unique. So if you have a friend, however he came to be one, it is well worth doing everything possible to maintain the relationship.

After a minor misunderstanding one evening, Marty's wife Elaine wrote me a conciliatory note expressing her concern that she may have overstretched the bounds of our relationship, since she was only a "derivative friend." By that she meant that Marty was my "real" friend, and she was just an appendage.

True, we would not have met except for Marty; we would probably not have become friends if Elaine had not married him. However, a friend is a friend regardless of how the relationship began—and I consider her my friend, without any qualifying adjective.

I feel that way about Phyllis, Dave, Midge, and Marge . . . Dalia, Paul, Irene, Evelyn, and lots of other friends and relations of other friends without whom we would have never met. And they are all my friends without qualification.

I have never met Hugh and Gayle face-to-face, although we often talk by telephone. They are "derivative friends" from Jerry. Yet I know that they are friends to me, and I hope I am one to them. When I was writing my last book I got stuck, and could not see any way out. My health was on the skids, and it looked like I might never have the energy to get it right.

Without the slightest hesitation they offered to edit the manuscript and make suggestions. This came at a time of great pressure for them, just having returned from traveling and faced with their own publication deadlines. However, they made time to help a friend they only knew by telephone.

How strange it is—I know so little about the stories of their lives. The fragments that I do know do not tell me much, but still I think of them as exemplary of friends.

Some of what I know about them seems almost funny, too.

From one of Hugh's books I discovered that Gayle has great legs. And because I have another friend who once attended a religious high school with Hugh, I learned he was expelled for prematurely healing others—before he had attained the proper credentials in the church. As fascinating as "great legs" and "premature healing" may be, this is very spare information to have about an important friendship. The only other information I have is that their children are central to their lives, for they have moved several times just to assure a healthful environment for them.

They probably know as little of me. Yet, even without a common history to hang it on, I feel I know them very well. For with their generosity, they have added meaning to my life. They willingly set their own formidable work aside to help a troubled friend. Would I have been that kind if the roles had been reversed? Perhaps not that time, but now I would, for I learned a vital lesson from what they did for me, and something vital about the nature of friendship.

I realize again that when you help a friend, it may be of immense significance to him, but not so important to you. In some mysterious way, you are also helping you, and together the two of you are as one. At those times, your friend's fate is also yours.

In a selfless act, you are serving a part of who you really are. And if you turn away a friend, you deprive yourself and are the loser, too, just like him. Exactly how that works I cannot say, but I repeatedly encounter evidence to support this truth. And that is how I feel with Gayle and Hugh, these people I have never seen. If I could be of use to them in some way, it would be as much for me as for them—one of the mysteries of friendship!

And that reminds me of Bob, my pal from Baltimore. We were introduced by minor acquaintances, and yet he has become a true and faithful friend. When I was first in charge of the community psychiatry program, I realized my ignorance of social theory. He was a sociology professor interested in my field, so I hired him to teach and guide me through the maze of sociology literature. Bob lived in California for only one year, however, that brief time set the stage for us to become friends and we have been ever since. Although we are now separated by a continent, he and Joan manage to spend some time with us each year. The entire burden of travel has been on them in recent years, since it is no longer possible for me to make the trip.

When we met, we hit it off immediately. Adversity had brought us together, and something indefinable kept us united. We are very different in so many ways, yet our relationship has grown and grown. It is fascinating to me how—despite different backgrounds—we have arrived at such similar outlooks.

One thing I know is that we laugh a lot when we are together, and share the same perverse sense of humor. His raucous laughter is so irresistible that even if I did not get the joke I would be forced to laugh. In every tragedy we have faced, and both of us have had our share of them, we find a little something that makes it funny. It has been a saving grace and continues to solidify our alliance.

He is someone with whom I feel free to say whatever is on my mind. He knows the best and worst, the weak and strong in me, and he is always available to let me know he cares. I learned much more than social theory from him, for there could not be a more accepting person than Bob. I have learned the meaning of unconditional love from him and he has made it clear that whenever I am in need, he will be there.

We have done some crazy things together or, I should say, he has made it possible for me to do them. He has carried me onto the most precarious rides at Disneyland, just by scooping me up. He has taken me on daring boat trips and a remarkable four-wheel-drive excursion. In his three-story Baltimore row house he carried me upstairs every night, and down each morning.

Since we both love to eat, especially seafood, we have lots of restaurant and kitchen adventures: to reach cafes, he has carried me up narrow stairways; we have struggled to crack the claws of a twenty-pound lobster; and once we were attacked by a bushel of enraged blue point crabs after the bottom of their container collapsed. When he and Joan visit from Maryland, they bring generous amounts of crabs, oysters, clams, and mussels.

I have made a minor contribution to our culinary adventures by being disabled and in a wheelchair. A favorite

Baltimore restaurant takes no reservations, so the line to get in is always long. However, they do take wheelchairs first, so at last, I have found an advantage to my handicap.

We have laughed often, and cried together. I look forward eagerly to seeing him; I have a lot to share. Several years ago, he left academia to become a family therapist, a perfect profession for his natural talents. There is so much I could say about him and his fine family, too much for the space I have here, but perhaps what is most telling is that I have been smiling while writing this.

The world can be a very lonely place. Friends can make it much less so. People who feel alone need not be lost, for as long as there are people, the possibility of friends exists. You may need to try repeatedly to open yourself to the possibility. It may require giving up a little self-aggrandizing pride, a long-held prejudice here or an intolerant judgment there, but it is worth the price when you can find the best in those who come your way.

Friendships tend to grow in depth and number with the first. If you make a single friend, others will soon be nearby, for they have friends of theirs. The process tends to grow exponentially: You bring one, then the other does, and that makes four.

If you compare each sunset with some ideal, you fail to see the one before your very eyes. All friendships differ, and none can be compared. If you expect your friend to be just the way you want, you are no friend. The question is, can you see the friend behind your differences? If not, you are not his friend. What you see on the surface will vary—the words they speak, their quirks and habits—but underneath, friends are much the same in one respect. You will know they are friends by that special feeling you have when with them, a familiar warmth and safety we all seek.

All friends are derivative friends, for they come from a common source. The immediate vehicle may not be the same: a mutual friend, your work, your church, your play, but the ultimate source from which they all emerge must be love.

FOURTEEN

From Work to Friendship: Helen O

Bring all people into friendship with you.
—Letter to Aristeas

OF ALL THE PEOPLE I know, there is no one with more goodwill towards everyone than Helen, and not because she has had it easy by any means. We worked together for years and, although we are roughly the same age, she retired before I did. She bought a tiny house in the sparsely populated high desert.

I had serious concerns about the move. As a gregarious person with many, many friends in Los Angeles, she might be bored and lonely in the desert, I thought. However, I underestimated the extent of her magnetic appeal. Within a year a number of her old friends had also moved nearby and she had made many new ones.

When you have so much love, other people want to share in it and find ways of coming into your life. I thought she would be lonely; however, very soon she was singing in the local choir, managing two bridge clubs, working a few hours a week as a consultant, serving on the county mental health advisory board, and lots more. I do not think she sought any of these—they came to her.

There are many people in the world who are lonely and hunger for more friends; they must wonder why friends come to her. I think I know! The secret is that she always reinforces the best in people and wants them to succeed. How does she do that? She respects and unconditionally supports other people's right to differences and rarely insists that her way alone is the best. Still, she often holds firm beliefs of her own.

She cares for nearly all people, and wants the best for them. These qualities make her a natural consultant to others. You never feel put down by Helen and usually you feel better and more worthwhile from time spent with her. So why would people not want to be with her?

Once, she and Rita and I had been together for a day. We were all trying unsuccessfully to remember the words to the song "Send in the Clowns." We ended up looking for a store that sold sheet music. When Rita pulled the van up to the curb on a crowded street, she scraped the fender of a parked sports car. We forgot the song, and Rita went to find the owner of the car. It took time, but finally she found out he worked in a nearby office. He was an automobile insurance agent who knew exactly how to handle the situation for himself!

She told him what she had done and was shocked to learn how much the repairs would cost. After that we were all feeling quite deflated. We remembered what our real mission was, but the enthusiasm was gone. Nevertheless, Helen went into the music store to see if she could find the sheet music.

Alas, they did not have it. But, before she had time to feel discouraged, a young couple who had overheard her ask for the song intervened. They said that they had the music and words at home and offered to make a copy for us. Pleased now, she returned to the van, where we were still feeling glum. She enthusiastically told us the good news.

Our moods were transformed, and good cheer returned. On the way home, I began to think about what had taken place. Rita had given no thought to anything but doing what was right and hadn't even considered escaping her responsibility. She treated the owner of the sports car with the same respect and concern she would a friend.

Although the financial price was high, we need not feel regret, for what she gave was returned in kind, although once removed. The generosity of the couple in freely supplying the song completed the circle of kindness and overshadowed the costs incurred. How fortunate, I thought, to be in the company of two such lovely, caring women.

"What goes around comes around" seemed to be what happened—some money was lost but friendship was the gain. Can it be mere coincidence? It has seemed that way so often: The response will come, although not as you might anticipate. Goodwill does seem to beget goodwill in the same way love produces love. And Helen and Rita were the emissaries, but exactly how it is transferred from one situation to another I do not know.

Love has always been important for Helen. She once gave me her copy of a translated Swedish novel. In Hjalmar Söderberg's *Doctor Glas,* the protagonist—in desperate search for love—observes, "We want to be loved; failing that, admired; failing that, feared; failing that, hated and despised. At all costs we want to stir up some sort of feeling in others. Our soul abhors a vacuum. At all costs it longs for contact."

So much of what we see in life is a distortion of that central need to feel contact and love. Helen knows, as we all must learn, that it must begin with you, and although it may be easier if you have received love first, the opportunity is always there.

Helen was born in Singapore to Swedish parents, and Swedish was the language she heard at home. Although she lived in the United States from childhood, as with everyone her childhood had its trials. A painful part was the realization that her parents never told her she was loved. In fact, the first awareness of the Swedish phrase for "I love you" came from seeing an Ingmar Bergman film.

Chris, a young Swedish man, has been the trusted mainstay for my personal care for several years. One day, to contrast the United States with Sweden, he mentioned offhandedly that the phrase *Jag alskar dej* (I love you) is almost never heard in Sweden and that parents would not say it to their children.

I wondered if some of Helen's feeling that her parents did not love her enough might have resulted from differences in cultural attitudes about the verbal expression of it. And would knowing this information be of help? She had grown up in America adopting the manners and expectations of her peers; although her parents lived in America, their attitudes and expressions were shaped a generation earlier and thousands of miles away in Sweden.

I called her immediately to tell her what I had learned. She was silent for a time and then observed that it was indeed helpful information, but so at variance with her lifetime mindset that it would take a long while to assimilate. And I know it does. But whatever forces may have shaped her views, she has never hesitated in her quest to provide her share in love.

Helen, somehow, learned to express love much more freely than her parents had been able. In breaking the cultural barriers she had inherited, she transcended the kind of miserly constrictions imposed on us. She reached beyond, to try to find the essence of what is human in us all.

The way I have described Helen may seem very one-sided and excessively altruistic, however it is an accurate portrayal of my experience with her. Does she have a darker side, unknown to me? Perhaps, since we all have many sides, but they are not ones I have seen.

I know that we are all capable of wrongdoing as well as good. And which side we show depends upon the person we are with. For some we are mean and base; for others we seem pure love. Hitler loved children, Clyde

Barrow loved Bonnie Parker, and Tomás de Torquemada no doubt loved God. Yet each was a cruel murderer of many innocents.

Perhaps *Doctor Glas* was right: Beneath all the corruptions of a lifetime's search, there is always love. Helen has used her life giving generously of herself. She was never content to only receive, but knew to give and get are much the same. The only choice we really have is to associate ourselves with love, even though it may be in sending it out without obvious return. We live in the matrix of what we give out, so when our attention is on sending out instead of receiving, the problem's often solved.

Helen worked with me at the community education and research center I had begun. I had heard that she might be interested in leaving her university teaching post, so I called her for an interview. She was youthful, trim and attractive, but what I noticed most was an appealing mixture of reticence and eagerness. I intuitively knew that she was someone to trust in this new venture. And I was never disappointed. She later told me she felt the same with me. Sometimes you just know.

I was very worried that the program, which had a shaky start, might not succeed. So, I was often difficult and demanding with those who worked there. Helen and I had our share of disagreements, but always worked them out with the program first in mind. She brought important strengths that I could not—stable support and consistent clarity. Together, with our contrasting styles the program grew and flourished.

And we had lots of fun. We had lunchtime potlock parties to celebrate all occasions—even if some of them had to be contrived. There were the usual birthdays and holidays, but we also found obscure events ranging from the Garlic Festival to pivotal events of the Franco-Prussian wars. We crammed a lot of tomfoolery into the lunch break—and, in the process, important business work was done as well. None of it would have been possible without Daisy, my extraordinary secretary who was often the engineer, if not always the architect of these events. Unfortunately, when the program grew beyond the small core of us, such events began to disappear. We never had a staff of more than thirty, but even that small number seemed to pass a critical size, beyond which informality no longer does the job.

As the center grew, Helen and I spent a lot of time together, planning and solving problems. She was efficient and conscientious, but never lost sight of the people for the goal. And in that, she has helped me to tell the chaff from wheat. With her, it seemed more like fun than work.

She became a major force in the development of community health programs. With her exposure at the national level, she became a respected member of prestigious boards. She had offers of important university and governmental positions, yet she always knew what was important to her and that had nothing to do with money or prestige. What counts with Helen is beyond social status and recognition, something that is known in the heart alone, and not the head—love.

FIFTEEN

The Dancing Rose

All night have the roses heard
The flute, viola, bassoon;
All night has the casement jessamine stirr'd
To the dancers dancing in tune . . .
—ALFRED, LORD TENNYSON

S HE LOOKED like a whimsical sprite, under five feet tall, very mild-mannered. She moved with the grace of the dancer she once was, and although she was sixty-two when I first met her, she looked decades younger.

Her appearance was at sharp contrast with her distinguished credentials. She had just taken early retirement from the university professorship she had held for thirty years. I met with her to discuss the possibility of her joining the faculty of a new educational and research center, for she was an acknowledged expert on a form of consultation that would be a part of the new curriculum.

We met at the faculty club of her university. I attempted to make some small talk as a way of getting acquainted, but she was clearly quite impatient with it. Although she was pleasant, she was not particularly friendly. She was very serious and businesslike.

Eventually we struck a deal, and we planned to co-teach a course, mainly my decision, because I thought it prudent to monitor her teaching in this new setting. As cautiously as this began, it ultimately led to a decade of joint teaching and a successful textbook, still in use today. But more importantly, it led to deep mutual respect, affection, and friendship.

We certainly were contrasting personalities. I am over six feet tall, and she is quite small. She moves with unusual grace, while I am confined to a wheelchair. She is very serious; I can see some humor in almost anything. I think in abstract terms, she in very concrete ones. She is twenty years my senior. So what was the chemistry that allowed us to become such steadfast friends?

She held deep unshakable convictions about her work —sometimes making her seem uncompromising. That actually served as a basis for engagement at a visceral level with me. For while we had disagreements, they were always with respect. She forced me to face how apparently contradictory points of view, each with merits, could form aspects of a larger truth. Our discussions were, as a result, always stimulating and productive.

A pattern developed when we taught together. We would meet for an hour or two before each session to plan. Gradually over time our discussions strayed until they included almost everything. I came to appreciate her more and more.

Always earnest, she often followed up with a call or a note after we had talked. On further reflection she had seen some additional aspect of our discussion. I came to look forward to her thoughtful "postmortem" observations, for they unfailingly added light to darkness. Those afterthoughts would complete what had been said, bringing our exchanges to a graceful end with nothing left undone. They then left her free to embrace whatever would come next.

She helped me to recognize the preciousness of time. She understood that the only time that can be fully grasped is that which is experienced at this very moment —the rest is fantasy, but a fragment of memory or a future plan, known in the head perhaps, but never in the marrowbone. And she was determined to make the most of her time, always choosing reverently what she did.

She taught, she traveled everywhere, she gardened, and she read. She was also not afraid to waste some time, if she chose. However she spent her time, she was completely present-involved, and never wishing she was somewhere else. When you spoke with her, there was no one else for her but you; if she went somewhere, there was no other place for her; when she worked, there was no other task but the one at hand. She always savored what she did, carefully and thoughtfully.

I know of two great influences in her life. The first was when, still in her teens, she attended a dance performance in her native Philadelphia given by a famous European dancer, Mary Wigman. It took place in a cavernous hall where the stage was gigantic. Yet the dancer chose to use only a three-foot area for her performance and showed remarkable ingenuity in that tiny space. Rose grasped the essence of that performance and it became a principle by which to live.

She learned that how much space one covers in life is far less important than how space is used. There will always be limits within which to live and work; the challenge is how to creatively use what space we have. One can dance with utmost grace and beauty in an area no bigger than oneself.

Rose has used whatever space she has with loving care —and she also adds wise choice and elegance to the application. What a lesson for me!

My body lives within a tiny space with immutable limits. Although my space may be confined, my creativity need not be; I, too, can dance with grace and care. The lesson that Rose learned so thoroughly has now become a principle for me.

The second great influence for Rose was her analysis with Otto Rank, one of the most famous disciples of Sigmund Freud and for many years one of his closest confidants. Rank broke away from Freud to express his great interest in creativity. In Rose he found a near ideal person for the furtherance of it. The lesson that she learned was like the one she learned in dance. However, from Rank she learned its application in the creative use of time, not space: Once again, it's not how much you have, but how you choose to use it.

What I learned from Rose about time was not only profound but useful. My disability has often immobilized me in bed for extended times. With nothing much to do, time would drag interminably, making a few minutes seem like an eternity. My inspiration has now become the dancer on that huge Philadelphia stage. My challenge is the same: to creatively use what time and space I have, however limited they may be.

I have discovered that eternity is also here and now, and when absorbed in the space I am in, I have no sense of passing time, fast or slow. When you cannot move, the challenge may be greater, but the task is still the same. And I have discovered some interesting ways to do it in my alien circumstance, sometimes creating tasks where none exist, sometimes going deep inside, but examining what is here with my every sense. I still have far to go to live that way all the time, but I think I may be getting there.

Although Rose has certainly had her share of recognition and fame, she has never sought them out. She recognized those impostors for what they were, transient artifacts of human mind. After retiring as a university professor, she chose to become an elementary school teacher's aide, just because it interested her. No doubt she would have been welcomed as the principal or a consultant to the teachers, but that is not what attracted her.

Money, power, and position were not her goal; participating with the children was. Participating in life's processes is what she loves. What she looked for in children was development and growth, and when she saw its fragile signs, she nurtured and enjoyed it.

Rose could be very firm, never harsh, not condemning

another's views, but absolutely clear about what and with whom she would participate—as she would say, to what she would "lend herself." She could only "loan" herself, never more than that. She knows how to say "no" as well as "yes."

A serious person, she sometimes thinks I am being serious when I am joking. If I make an outrageous statement, she is very likely to consider it gravely, and then quite methodically express her differences. When she finally realizes it's a joke, she smiles benevolently, and acknowledges that she is sometimes too serious. She says she has learned from me to take some things more lightly.

Among her most endearing qualities is that in her seriousness she allows each encounter with another person to affect her deeply. Nothing someone says or does is insignificant, and every conversation has depth. This is the source of her continuous growth, even in her later years. If she has learned something from me, I am very pleased, because I have learned so much from her.

Now she is eighty-five. She lives with her dear friend Irene in a retirement home. She has had two strokes that have slowed her down. When I saw her recently, however, she seemed the same as ever. She spoke of strokes in terms of what she had learned from them and from her recent hospitalizations.

Although her speech is somewhat slowed, the same intense involvement in life is present. She is as sensitive and respectful as she has always been. While her tiny feet still remain firmly planted on the ground and in the present moment, her gaze is focused on what comes next. She and Irene are planning some trips, even while recognizing the frailty of her health.

She says I am her friend, and when she says it, I feel the impact heavily. She does not say things casually and I doubt that many people would qualify as friends for her. I have been her boss, her teaching colleague, her student . . . and she even may have learned a thing or two from me. But what pleases me most is that I am, indeed, her friend.

SIXTEEN

It Is Never Too Late to Make a Friend: Bud

After the age of forty there isn't much to live for except friendship. —FRANCINE DU PLESSIX GRAY

CONVENTIONAL WISDOM tells us that the older you get, the more difficult it is to make new friends. I think it is true only if you are no longer in a position to meet new people. My mother found that by the time she reached eighty, she had sadly outlived nearly all of her old friends. However, with effort, she was able to make new ones—some who became very close —by going to a senior citizens' center and attending night school.

But now, ten years later, they too have died, and my mother can no longer drive her car, has much difficulty walking, and has insufficient energy to get to the places where she might meet more new friends. Still, she has persisted in trying through the organizations with which she does have contact—those offering transportation and other services to elders who are homebound. Some of the people whom she meets only by telephone nevertheless recognize her warmth and generosity, and come to visit in her home. Still she tries, and by now has befriended her neighbors on the street. But they are young, spend their time at work, and with their growing families.

So, alas, most of the time she is alone, without the energy to get out to make new friends or visit the few that do remain. And that takes its toll, for she thrives on friends and human contact. Since Rita and I live sixty miles from her, we want her to live with us, or at least nearby. She has always taken pride in her independence, and insists that she will not leave her own home until she is carried out.

She comes to stay with us, two or three times a month. Often she seems to have lost her verve and interest for want of friends. After a few days, the stimulation here makes her come alive again. Then, as soon as she feels stronger and more optimistic, she misses her customary home, and insists it is time to leave again. What she needs are some friends nearby.

I am only sixty-four, and am fortunate that my old friends are mainly still around. However, my mobility and energy is no more than it might be for someone very, very old, and I do not get out much. I no longer meet new friends through work, and since my recreation is severely curtailed, I am lonely sometimes too.

I hate to burden friends with my needs, especially if mine are great. I like to feel that I pull my own weight and I feel unworthy when I don't. In this I am my mother's son. However, sometimes my needs *are* greater than my friend's and I am unsure of how much of them I dare to show. I do not wish to need too much. It would destroy my image of myself, so my pride conflicts with need.

If I were to ask for what I want, I could be refused, or even worse, my friend might have to make sacrifices for me. Then surely I would lose my precious self-esteem. If help is offered spontaneously, I think, my pretense of strength and illusions of pride can remain intact. But as great as it may feel when a friend is sensitive, and intuitively responds to my needs, it is not a very good test of friendship. A need that has not been expressed is too easily misread and an offer of help can too easily be out of phase with it.

If my need is present, why should I not express it with friends? And if they should feel compromised by what I ask, why should they not say "no"? After all, one of the qualities most prized in friends is their honesty.

Friends can respond as friends without meeting my every need as I might wish. Even if they do not do what I ask, they can show their friendship in their response and they will be concerned with my finding other means to meet my needs.

To have and be a friend, you cannot be bound by some self-imposed protocol. Whoever it was that said friendship requires fifty-fifty giving was wrong. In true friendship nobody counts who gives what or how much—that would be a business deal. Although it might be convenient if it worked out that way, among good friends, each is willing to give 90 percent, if not 100 percent of what they can.

You can usually recognize a friend by feel: You feel good when they are near and, when they are not, they remain alive within the heart. You know a friend when you know it is *you* who care. Mother Teresa is a friend to everyone, for it matters not to her if "friends" respond at all. Does this suggest that, when you ask the question—"Are you a friend to me?"—you may be limiting how much the relationship can grow?

To find a friend, a person must first have a means to look for one, and that may challenge your creativity. Then, you must treat those you meet as though they were already your friends—with care, concern, and generosity, thinking more of what you can give than get. And if you can find some common links with them, friendship may then become a true reality.

I first met Bud because we are both old polios, with diminishing abilities to breathe. We had been using portable chest-shell respirators at night, but they had become inadequate. I tried breathing by holding a tube in my mouth attached to a respirator; however, I could not fall asleep with it, so had to go back to sleeping in an iron lung.

Bud and his wife, Dalia, had heard erroneously that I was successfully using the tube-in-mouth method that he, too, had tried without success. They came to visit and share the struggles with another who understood—not the blind, but the lame leading the lame. Eventually we both abandoned the mouth method in favor of a mask covering the nose which holds the respirator tube. Although we have had some success, we still seek "a better nose to live by."

Out of this collaboration we have become friends. We speak on the telephone every day, and share more and more. Dalia magnanimously offered to type the final manuscript for my book *Flying Without Wings,* which was not an easy job, but one she completed with efficient results. Together Bud and Dalia, who are computer buffs, have indoctrinated me into that useful world, and when I first began, I shamelessly called on them for help. And they were always available.

I have known them only about three years, but our friendship has grown very firm. With Bud, I feel I can give as well as get, and neither of us is compromised. The other night, quite late, my new respirator stopped working. Knowing that Bud had a similar one for a much longer time, I called. He did know what to do, and soon it was working once again. To my surprise, I had called at what could have been an awkward hour, with little hesitation. How strange for me to be so bold.

But Bud and Dalia said, "If it stops again, call at any time," and offered their spare respirator as well. Their unfailing generosity makes it much easier for me to ask. And I also know that Bud feels free to call on me, allowing me to feel more equal and less burdensome.

We are recent and late-life friends, yet important ones. We have mutual interests and, I think, both feel understood (although we don't necessarily always agree). We have lived remarkably different lives, yet come together in mutuality.

I would like to believe that time is not important in friendship, but with new friends there are some differences. In *Friends and Friends of Friends,* John Leonard says, "It take a long time to grow an old friend," and I agree. Bud and I almost immediately shared very intimate, personal things and from the beginning I considered him an important friend.

But, to my surprise, I realize that I am often testy with him and he with me. In getting close so quickly, we had bypassed time, and a relationship that forms without resistance cannot last. People are different, and those differences must be negotiated. It takes some time to reach a true accommodation and if it is not done at first, then the issues will come up later.

Nevertheless, many Americans try to instantly appear as though they are intimate friends with everyone. But, no substantial friendship can develop without some trials and some time. Bud and I are in the process of catching up with the resistances we missed at first. And we will, because the value of the friendship is clear and we have commitment to it.

It is never too late in life to try being a friend. Your creativity may be challenged to find some common meeting ground, but, as long as communication is possible, new friendships can become a reality.

I know a woman who cannot speak because of a brain tumor. Nevertheless, she has made good new friends of people who come to her house to help for various reasons. Her difficulty in communication would seem to make new friends impossible, but it has become the very vehicle for involvement with others, as they are challenged to respond and understand.

Another woman, in a rural southern town, was paralyzed and could not go out of her house. She missed having friends, so whenever she heard of someone on radio or TV whom she would like to know, she would try to call them. And sometimes she developed friendships. Because she lived on public welfare and had so little money with which to make the calls, she would often have her telephone friends call her.

So it is never too late to make new friends, for relating is what people can do best. There are always others out there who are in need as well as you, and if you can discover the way in which their needs and yours are complementary, you will probably have a fine new friend.

SEVENTEEN

Kinship and Friendship: Those Who Help for Pay

We need old friends to help us grow old and new friends to help us stay young. —LETTY COTTIN POGREBIN

MY DISABILITY mandates that people be available to help me all day and night. Amazing Rita efficiently managed my needs during the first twenty-five years of our marriage, enabling us to do almost everything other married couples could, including extensive travel. Then, as we grew older, my needs grew while her strength diminished, making this arrangement more difficult.

About ten years ago, Rita, who could easily have been a model for a health and beauty magazine, developed disabling rheumatoid arthritis. Now, along with all the other things we have shared in nearly forty years together, we have disability, and disability makes us continuously aware of how slender is the thread which separates life from death. So I wonder what we will leave behind.

The people we hire to help have generally been quite young. Often, even if they may not know it, they are in transition between leaving their families and developing their own independent lives. Our household is a temporary way station. And we see them at their best and worst. They lurch between dependence and autonomy, usually overshooting the mark one way or another, so it is not always smooth or easy.

Neither is it easy to deal daily with different people helping with my most intimate bodily functions. And there is never any respite. But it appears one of our tasks is helping these young people on their way, while they help me. So we have learned to roll with the punches, and there are many rewards as well.

Those who help for pay become our friends. There have been many by now—black and white and brown and yellow; Protestant, Catholic, Jewish, Moslem, and Buddhist. And we remain in touch with almost all. Some are in their forties by now, while others are still in school.

Three are doctors, and two more are on their way. There are several businessmen, a psychologist, a journalist, a bodybuilder/craftsman, a real estate developer, an attorney, two teachers, and a health service planner. We have witnessed and participated in their weddings, divorces, births, and such. There is even a young Arnold in the world named for me (the baby would have been a Rita, if it had turned out to be a girl).

Although Rita and I passionately engaged in all the usual activities to produce offspring, we were blessed with none. Rita's desire for children was always unreserved, but I had my doubts, not knowing how long I would live. That no longer matters, though; the fact is that we will never pass our genes on to children who will survive us.

I had a second chance to live after I was paralyzed, different than the way I lived before, but rewarding just the same. And that seems the way with children too—I got a second chance, although not the usual way. The young people who help me become like my children. We participate in their lives in important ways, and they in ours. We develop intimate relationships, and talk of almost everything. They often say that they can talk with us in ways they could not talk at home. Perhaps we are to them what Louise and Clyde and Fritz were to me—very special older friends, who seem wise in the world's ways.

They provide us with care, and we care about them. We share in their experiences, aspirations, disappointments, and regrets. Although not included in the original agreement, they get some of Rita's gourmet cuisine as an extra. We have our fights and disagreements; we negotiate and usually make up. When they move away they stay in touch, and when they don't, we are apt to worry. I guess you would call them friends.

Is friendship different when there is pay involved? I am sure it is, for at first, it is the basis for exchange. There have been only one or two with whom relationships never moved beyond the business stage. With them, the fit was just not right. For most, what may have begun as a simple business pact soon became a bargain for us all.

Friendship always begins as something else, some arrangement that brings people together where they can meet. It begins in many different ways, and only later can you really know if it has jelled. (Even when the explicit reason for meeting others is friendship, as with singles' clubs, personal ads, or dating services, there is no more success than when meeting ostensibly for other reasons. If you are a friend, you will find some friends, wherever you may meet).

We give our helpers advice sometimes, solicited or not. We feel free in doing that, for we all know that they, like us, are free to use it (or not) as they may wish. Rita and I know we don't have the hold on them that perhaps their families do. For we are friends, and friends are free.

No, we do not have children; other people did that for us. But we are participants in the flow of life, and can see the future in these youngsters' eyes. We care about how they fare in life, and hope we can help them reach their goals.

And how wonderful these children/friends are! Their diversity provides us with a window on the whole world —we have the joy of intimately participating in the lives of children from so many different cultures and lands.

There is Frank, who lived with us for two fulfilling years while studying for an M.B.A. Now married, living in the Midwest, we have been with him, in our way, through his marriage, his having children. His wife Charlotte worked for six months while Frank stayed home to experience full-time parenting and househusbandry; then they switched again, with him at work, and her at home —what a marvelous experience! He has tried some different jobs, from corporate life to educator—competent at them all; his search was not so much for success, as for experience and meaning. And we have also shared their beginning quest to find a religious framework within which to place it all, as we vicariously travel on the journey with them.

And we have been through the ups and downs, and ins and outs with Bob and John, Chris and Don, Earl and Gordon, Dan and Alex, David and Jeff. Sometimes they may fade from our lives, but never from our memories. And just about the time we think they are gone for good, to our surprise they may reappear (as it was with my very first friends, the Buddies).

We have come to know the world through them, and even some of what lies beyond. They are the future, and we can see some hope. If they will have a part in its design, there is good reason for optimism. They represent the best in the America that is yet to come. The values they embrace are also ours: diversity, yet respect and kindness for all; the desire and will to make a better world. They know that their fate is not in isolation, but must be in accord with family, community, society, the world, the universe. They seek to befriend it all, and we are proud to have a share.

Many people today are voluntarily choosing not to have children. Unfortunately, those who make that choice are often the most competent and educated members of our society. They think it would be cruel to bring a child into such a polluted, crime-, drug- and corruption-ridden world, faced with declining ozone-layer protection, and the threat of nuclear war, not to mention overpopulation and deforestation. Some people are more interested in their careers, and do not believe that they have the time for posterity.

We are senior citizens now, and increasingly aware that our individual lives on earth are coming to an end. Our connections with other humans (not necessarily biologically related), as well as connections with all things in the universe, seem ever more precious. I am ever more aware of friends and friendship, and the relationship between friendship and biological kinship.

When the human world was young, kinship meant everything. Who your parents and family were determined what you would be. Survival as an individual depended on being a member of a group, so the individual was subordinate to that group. Banishment was a punishment worse than death, for it included both disgrace and the likelihood that a person could not survive alone.

It is very unlikely that people even thought of themselves as unique or individual because the tribal bonds were so strong. A few, like chiefs or wise men, had certain special powers for the whole group; however, most other people were very much alike, sharing all of the same experiences and influences.

By comparison, the bonds in American families today are generally not very strong, and as near as we usually get to clans are "gangs." Divorce, remarriage, one-parent families or both parents working, the decline of authority and the diminishing influence of religious values have all occurred at the same time that people have begun to think of themselves as individuals apart from a community. One may well have also caused the other, but it is impossible to know.

People today have more freedom to choose where they live, what they do for work or play, and who they spend their time with. They try out different things, people, and life-styles. They move around a lot, and have different sources of information—books and newspapers, television and radio, computers, videos and movies—that also make them different individually.

Psychological concepts often become popular movements, and provide values for people. But the values often inferred from "assertiveness training" and "winning by intimidation" and "co-dependency" are that we are all alone, and survival is entirely an individual matter and concern. We are freer to choose in every way, and at younger ages. So it is no surprise that as individuals, each person feels as if he or she is at the center of the universe, and beholden to fewer and fewer people.

These changes are neither bad nor good, but a fact of life, part of an evolutionary trend. I must confess nostalgia for how things were, and the stability that I once knew. But the clock cannot be turned back, and besides, the price of the old stability was constriction, and quite suffocating. There were not many choices that could be made when families set all the rules.

There were other problems with the close family among the ancients; for example, all family members were equally culpable. If only one of them committed a crime, all members of the family and the clan shared guilt equally—"bloodguiltiness," it was called. Each member was sentenced prior to birth for a crime of which they had no firsthand knowledge—hardly our view of justice today.

People could not rise above their station, their caste or class. They were stuck with what they had at birth. Those seem like very barbaric and unenlightened views today— not at all suited to the contemporary view of personal responsibility, which we believe far more just.

Crippled though families may be, they remain essential, but they are not the only force supporting and shaping people's lives: peer groups, television, radio, movies, and school environments all play important roles. Troubled children could once be clearly traced to trouble in the family; it is no longer necessarily the case. The family cannot flourish without coherent community support, and not much is offered. Is blood still "thicker than water" today, or is it just "stickier"?

This is where friendship comes in—as the most important free choice made. Although important bonds still exist within families, relationships from the community determine how strong they are, and support or undermine them. Through friendship, community links are forged, and the support we need comes from friends.

We are all in this world together, whatever our family or clan, and the fate of one affects us all. We need to see beneath the surface to find the basic similarities between ourselves and others. If we can restore connections, then as individuals we can serve our common destiny.

Whether we like it or not, if we blow up our enemies, we destroy ourselves. And if the planet becomes so polluted that it is uninhabitable, no individual will have a place to live. If, as Vince Lombardi said, "Winning is the only thing," together we all can win, but not as individuals alone. Whether Iraqis or Iranians, Irish Protestants or Catholics, Moslems or Christians or Jews, or whites or blacks, we had all better discover how to befriend each other, other species, the planet on which we live—before there is nothing left.

When strangers first came out of the forest and shook hands, it was not to show friendship, but to check for weapons. They carried cloths of white to show there was no blood. So even the most self-protective gesture may become a symbol of friendship, and strangers can, with effort, make friends of enemies.

"Family ties" can include the whole family of man, beyond simple biology and genes. They may include the conscious choice of friends, if we can only see we have common interests and basic mutual strivings. We must live together in these times of need, to become familiar with one another's ways. Kinship and friendship both require familiarity and longevity.

Although I would not have freely chosen it, I feel fortunate that I require so much help. For in my relationships with those I pay for aid, I have seen a microcosm of the future I hope will come.

EIGHTEEN

Time, Money, and Friendship

Who looks for a faultless friend will have none.
—LAZEROV

MANY YEARS AGO, while I was still in my psychiatric training, I was in group therapy. It was a very gratifying experience, with a charismatic leader and a fine group of individuals. Powerful feelings surfaced and a deep bond developed among the members. One day, after many previously guarded memories and feelings were revealed, a passionate sense of intimacy engulfed the group. Tears were shed as one member after another spoke movingly of how much their "sharing" with the group had meant. Although, I felt the same way, the word "sharing" seemed discordant, and echoed through my head.

With the crazy kind of insight that often emerges in such groups, I blurted out that to say we were sharing was meaningless, for we shared only within an already accepting forum, and that what we shared was no more than personal hidden ghosts. "Now, the real test of sharing," I continued, "would be for each of us to bring all our money and share it." Silence reigned, and everyone

Time, Money, and Friendship 195

looked at me aghast. My brutish comments had broken the magic bond. It was, of course, thoughtless insensitivity on my part, but like all such things it held a grain of truth. Money is something that is rarely shared easily.

Recently I was visited by a remarkable man, a university professor, physician, and former Olympic rowing gold medalist. Born in Europe, he was a guerrilla partisan, who fought against the Nazi invasion. He was captured, starved, and tortured; now in his twilight years, he was in constant pain from accumulated disabilities. Despite all of these trials, he had only a single complaint: that although he had been here over thirty years, he had no true friends in the United States.

At a party in his honor, a thousand people came to celebrate. He had legions of acquaintances who considered him a friend; he was much esteemed and widely praised, the recipient of lofty prizes. But there was no one he would truly call his friend, like the friends he knew in Europe. The difference, he said, was *money,* and Americans value it more than they do friends!

My reaction was to defend my friends and country; I wanted to protect the integrity of my friendships. I told him of many instances of generosity when friends have touched my life with gifts as valuable as cash. He was unconvinced, and said, "The friends you describe gave surplus funds, and they did not feel a pinch themselves; true friends give things to you that they need just as much themselves." His examples were a last morsel of food, or the last dollar.

196   *The Only Gift*

So I told him about Jerry, who had completely stopped charging people for his medical services, and freely gave away what money he had to those in need. But the man still looked at me with skepticism. I realized he would not be convinced . . . and then, I thought, "Convinced of what?" Of what was I trying to persuade him?

We may well be a nation that overvalues money, yet I doubt that Europeans are more generous with friends than Americans. Perhaps there are countries where the social structure diminishes the importance of money, and the individual does not require much of his own. What little a person might have could then be given away without deprivation.

Even if he was right, in most cases the test of friendship he had chosen was irrelevant. Of course his youthful friends in Europe would willingly share what they had with a friend: It was very little sacrifice. They were young, healthy, and without family responsibilities. For them to give away all of their material possessions to help a friend would deprive no one else. No, his test of friendship was hardly a fair one.

I love my friends today, and would do everything possible to help them. My responsibilities to family are also obligations that only I can carry, and they may take precedence. I would not want to choose between a friend and, let's say, my wife, whom I deeply love and to whom I owe prime responsibility. That would be no choice at all. It may have been a task for a Solomon, not for me. More important, though, is that to expect a friend to make such a choice, means you are no friend.

Yet, perhaps this wasn't my visitor's point. Rather, he may have meant that too often money separates us from love. How often does money produce the differences between people, and just as sad, how often is it the glue that keeps them together? I have no doubt that evangelists Jim Bakker, Jimmy Swaggart and Oral Roberts once loved both man and God. But too much money and the power it brought tore them from their love.

As a physician and psychiatrist, I am one who helps others for pay, so it is only fair to ask "Are my patients also friends?" Certainly, they come to see me expecting something else . . . to rid themselves of symptoms, to resolve a crisis, to develop more satisfying relationships or to discover how to achieve some goal.

The fundamental purpose of our work determines the structure of our relationship and limits how free we are to act with one another. I will try to keep the focus on what we have agreed upon as the goals and keep in mind the meaning and significance of any time either of us should stray from them. I expect nothing but whatever fee we have agreed upon.

However, beyond all of the therapeutic techniques, ethical considerations and the money, a deep level of intimacy develops that is anything but neutral for me. I care very deeply for my patients, yes, lovingly. They add meaning to my life and teach me things I need to know. That I call them "patients" instead of "friends" seems quite arbitrary to me.

Of course I do not care equally about all of them, but the depth and quality of feelings are similar to those with my other friends. If it were not that I must make a living, I would gladly work with them for free and I would never stop working with a patient who was unable to pay.

"Time is money," it is said, but although time may have some relationship with money, it is certainly not the whole story. For neither money nor time have any permanence. Money may be held temporarily, sometimes for years, but time is only for an instant, and can never be held. That instant cannot be prolonged by money, no matter how much of it one possesses. A billionaire has no more time than a pauper.

If you hold onto money, in time its value usually decreases with inflation. However, the longer you keep a friend, the more his value grows, and old friends are treasured most of all. I think time is more nearly like friendship, for when you bask in the love of friends, the time together has few bounds. Its value cannot be measured; loving friends are true wealth.

My mother is over ninety years old, and she is very frail. Recently she attended a banquet at which I was being honored. I was alarmed when I saw her, for she seemed quite out of touch with what was going on, and barely seemed to notice when I spoke to her. She did not respond when I asked her if she was all right. "Is she ill?" I wondered.

Time, Money, and Friendship   199

Afterward, Rita and I brought her home with us. In the car on the way she seemed more alert, and finally said, "I had the strangest experience. I was not alone at the banquet; I kept seeing Dad [my father], and it was as though we were talking together, as we used to do. And my friends were there—Mary, Frances, Melvina, Fritzy, and all the others, and we were talking, too.

"We were talking about all the things we used to do, and how proud we were of you and Stan [my older brother, who is also gone]. Nothing like that ever happened to me before." She looked at me as though in awe.

"Was it pleasant?" I asked.

"Oh yes," she said, "we were together again!"

My mother has always said that when she dies, she will join all of those she loved who have gone before her. I do not know how that works, but who is to say she won't? Certainly not me!

Her experience adds another dimension to the timelessness of love and friendship. Although those who meant so much to her are now dead, they do remain alive within her. Perhaps, in some strange way we cannot comprehend, she also lives in them, wherever they may be.

My mother's experience makes me wonder at how enduring loving friendships can be. She believes without a doubt that friends and friendships continue in some other plane after they are gone from earthly time. What she sees is not the same as my vision, but she is closer to that next plane than I am.

I am no mystic, and I take pride in rationality. But the

essence of a rational position is to accept what we do not know. There is so much of which we are unsure. Perhaps someday a method for understanding the great unknown will be found. In the meantime, it would be wise not to be too sure.

But whatever belief you have, it's safe to say that a true friendship has very strong qualities of endurance. They have a way of extending beyond the bounds of simple time, and the older one becomes, the more those conventional boundaries disappear.

On earth we think that development of age is a loss of capacity, signaling death. But each loss also has some gain, if we can only get beyond the grief we feel. When he was in his nineties, William James was asked if he believed there was life after death. He replied that he didn't believe it very much until recently. It seemed to him he was "just becoming fit to live." But, live where? For in earthly terms, he was growing weaker by the day. Perhaps, the gain he felt was in his ability to become a good and close friend to those he loved, but were now gone.

To find explanations for friendship, people usually refer to what can be understood: "We have known each other since we were children"; We completely understand each other"; We have so many common interests"; We are so much alike"; or simply, "We can always depend on each other."

However, friendship does not ultimately depend on mutual advantage. And it does not depend on common interests or how long people have been acquainted. It does not even depend on helpfulness, frequent contact, or association—often months, even years may intervene between meetings. These verbal explanations are no more than oversimplifications that allow us to comphrend what would otherwise seem ineffable. Yet friendship is something that transcends life's details.

Friendship elevates the plane of human experience, to where we no longer feel alone or in conflict. We are able to look beyond differences with our friends to see something more fundamental, something which reminds us of what we seek with all of our worldly strivings. In friendship we find simultaneous feelings of peacefulness and stimulation, of harmony and individuality, of unity without sacrificing separateness.

If I trace my own capacity to be a friend, from my birth to who I am today, it has grown each year. With Louise and Clyde and the Buddies, I did not have much love to give, although I gave all I knew. But I am much better at it now. Perhaps that capacity will end on the day I die. Yet maybe, as my mother believes, the bounds of time will be extended to include the friends and love that have now vanished from this earth.

NINETEEN

From Friendship
to Universe

The bird a nest, the spider a web, man friendship.
—WILLIAM BLAKE

A FRIEND told me the other day that most of his friends appeared to be very different from him. He said he thought they overtly expressed parts of himself that were hidden, and he did the same thing for them.

He is seemingly a very reserved person, who carefully weighs whatever he will say before he speaks. One of his best friends, by contrast, impulsively blurts out whatever comes to mind, and prides himself on always "telling it like it is." His uncontrolled friend called one day and angrily complained, "You have not called me in two weeks, and I don't like it! It makes me feel as if our friendship has meaning only to me." Then, continuing without a pause, "Let's have dinner tonight."

My friend would never intrude that way, and would never be so demanding. But he feels liberated when his friend expresses what he would never do. When he hears what the demanding child within him would like to say, it makes him feel better about himself, and more nearly whole. He feels comfortable and at ease in the presence of his friend's openness.

This is true with some of my friends, too, and must be the reason I feel so free with them. We are opposites in many ways, yet we feel at ease together. Maybe I express overtly a part of them that has no voice as well. That may be the reason that, when they read my descriptions of our relationship, they were sometimes quite surprised.

Big Jim's bluntness contrasted sharply with my often cautious tactfulness. Marty's pride in being Jewish was quite unlike my own ambivalence. I thought that the way Jerry was teased would be fun, but I now know it caused him great pain. He thought I had great ease with girls, while I actually felt very awkward. Could what each of us saw have been a hidden part of ourselves instead? I do know that my association with them has helped me grow and acquire a bit of what they had already.

Friends often become our teachers. And because we are much the same in other ways, we learn that who we are is not so bad. From friends we also gain more self-acceptance and self-respect. I am more direct because from Marty I gained more appreciation of my origins, and Jerry has given me greater sensitivity.

With each friend one thing has remained the same. All of them, I am pleased to say, saw at least the same degree of bond with me that I do with them. However, what symbolized our relationship was often very different, and our memories might not be the same. No wonder nearly every one who read what I have written here found mystery in friendship.

Recently I visited with Barbara after a nearly forty-year hiatus. We talked about the times we had spent together with the kind of candor only possible because it was so long ago. We both recalled the same moonlit night at a beautiful coastal spot, but recalled sharply contrasting versions of that romantic scene.

In mine, my clumsy amorous moves were indignantly rebuffed by her. Her memory was that my failure to make a pass left her in dismay. What we shared in common was the unexpressed belief that "There must be something wrong with me." And the memory we each retained of other times contained similar discrepancies.

Entrapped in narrow self-preoccupation, what prisoners we all are! The connections we feel with friends must exist well beyond such limitations of thought and memory, and these connections make the attempts to describe the significance of friendship fall short. Yet beyond cognition, in our hearts, we hold the truth of what they are to us.

When babies are born, they cannot survive alone, making abandonment equivalent to death. The vestiges of that vulnerability remain deep within us throughout life. However, only in moments of acute awareness do we become conscious of the power of the fear, for we dedicate our lives to forging protections against it. We deny our vulnerability lest we become overwhelmed by terror.

If we can simply be loved and remain in blissful union,

we think there may be a chance. If we doubt that we can be loved, we look for other means to compensate; we seek power, money, prestige, and fame. When these, too, seem impossible, in desperation some make themselves hated and despised by committing awful deeds, in the cheerless hope that even a despicable notoriety is better than being forgotten and alone.

Friendship is our most successful antidote to that awful loneliness. George Herbert observed, "Life without friends; death without a witness." In friendship there is an experience of union. "What is a friend?" asked Aristotle. "A single soul dwelling in two bodies" was his response.

When I am with my friend, I need nothing more. All my desperate strivings recede into insignificance. A Latin proverb says that "Friends are thieves of time," and when I am with a friend, there is no time, only this moment in eternity.

I have always wanted to feel useful, so when I deem the things I do worthwhile, I feel good. Seeing my patients and helping them makes me feel valued. So does reaching others by writing what I hope will be of use. Each time I contribute to someone beyond myself I feel a sense of satisfaction. Are all these strivings just defenses . . . to keep from an awareness that I am alone?

I do know that when I am with a friend, I am not so compulsively ambitious, I am fulfilled and need nothing more. Robert Louis Stevenson must have felt as I do, for he said, "No man is useless while he has a friend." I no longer "must" do other useful things when I am with a friend; I am already useful, and restored to the oneness that I seek without all those other efforts.

But, there is a paradox here: Would I be worthy as a friend if I were not what I am, and did not want to be of use to others? Again, the way to have a friend is to be a friend. With my friends, their needs are also usually mine, so what I do for them is no sacrifice; it is just a part of me.

Henry Miller described friendship this way: "When I say friends, I mean friends. Not anybody and everybody can be your friend. It must be someone as close to you as your skin, someone who imparts color, drama, meaning to your life. . . . A life without friends is no life, however snug and secure it may be."

Every plant and animal along the evolutionary scale, from the lowliest bacteria to the greatest whale, is capable of biologically reproducing itself, so there is nothing unique about people being members of a family. But in friendship we transcend the limits of biology to see connections beyond our personal heredity. In friendship, we can see a part of us in unrelated others—the first essential leap with the potential to unite us to each and every thing on the earth and even with the stars beyond.

A person can, of his own free will, choose another person for what may become an intensely meaningful relationship, and that bond may be as close or even closer than family. Love of family is a virtue and an essential value, but friendship may be more important to the survival of mankind as a species. Only when in each act there is some concern for the needs of non-family others, do we have any chance at all. That is where friendship shines past the limits of biology. It leads farther than the obvious connections to the very substance of the universe and what is spiritual, the first essential link to God.

A child first depends entirely on its mother, then family, and only later, on friends. The circle of relationships tends to extend farther and farther beyond its limited origins as one grows older; yet it may be arrested at any stage, and is usually incomplete. Awareness that begins so narrowly may ultimately reveal relationships to everything seen, or touched, or felt. Just as species development expands from one cell to many in increasingly elaborate patterns, so does the consciousness of an individual, until we achieve an awareness of connections with the universe.

Another aspect of an evolution of consciousness begins with awareness of "good and bad." As we grow, we recognize that these primitive distinctions are only arbitrary and manmade, and that both aspects are present in almost everything, depending on the point of view. So we can choose the view we want to see—not ignoring the presence of the other, but subordinating it to the choice we have made.

This is not to deny the danger, cruelty, and evil we meet, lurking ever-present in the world. When they threaten us we must protect ourselves, but we need not be on guard all the time; if we are, we also miss the opportunities to find and make some friends. When there is even a tiny opening and we see any trace of an olive branch, we can reach out and nurture it, and it may bear fruit. We cannot control the world and we may fall victim at any time, but we can maximize the chances of creating the kind of place in which we want to live.

The idea of "best friends" is also an artifact of rudimentary human thought. At first, we are lucky if we have just one. As we mature, we find that having one does not keep us from having others of equal value, too. The belief that there can be only one best friend is transitional to a capacity to have more and deeper friendships. When we have developed the talent to be fully what we are and be fully open to another—with anyone—at any point in time, we achieve the ultimate maturity. Then we have the ingredients to be a best friend with anyone; the family of concern is no longer limited to the immediate family of our birth.

We begin our lives centered completely in ourselves, and awareness goes little beyond the skin. In the belief there is not enough for two, "me and mine" are the only things that count. Our viewpoint is "me not you," and "mine not yours." The world begins to change when we first make a friend; for then it becomes "me and you," but still me first. Then as we grow some more, we begin to see that fates are linked and, in certain ways, we are all the same.

As we grow and the world evolves, the center of the universe moves outward from inside our skins, to include other people, other things, and sometimes everything. And then we begin to realize that the seat of our souls is not inside the breath, the heart, the brain, or any other part of us. As the poet Novalis declared, it resides, "between you and me." Then, no longer just an objective "it," distorted by my stunted growth, the you becomes a "thou," a person just like me.

It is through our friends that we begin to make these discoveries. Each friendship is unique, and each friend shows us different aspects of who we are by who we are together with them. While we each appear to stand apart and separate, each of us reveals a special tiny bit of the whole. So we desperately need each other to catch a glimpse of what the world is really like. No choice need be made about what is just for me and what is just for you. Although our small needs dominate at any time, in the larger scheme, yours are as important as mine.

Each friendship has supported me to see more of what I knew before. As my friends, Louise and Clyde were more like another set of parents in the outer world. They helped give me birth into the world beyond my immediate family. Don and John, the twins, first showed me that I could find brothers outside my home. Big Jim then gave depth to my freely chosen brotherhood of friends.

Marty was my ethnic twin; in becoming friends with him I gained new trust in my own identity. Soulmate Jerry brought enduring love into focus as our connections grew. My capacity to see the affiliation beyond the few friends I had chosen was broadened and enhanced, when in serendipity other friends appeared to fill some empty need. Friends of friends who became my friends expanded

my boundary of inclusion even more. When Helen and Rose became my freely chosen sisters, they helped to further reduce my limits in the friendship bond.

With Bob I am completely free. And Bud and Ted showed me other dimensions: It is never too late to make a friend, and a friendship that has been lost can be regained. The young people who work for me extend the links of love and friendship across time and generation. And dear old Fritz gave the whole network coherent form. These and my other friendships extend the boundaries of time and space to reveal that it is all within my "I," and all that limits the circle of intimate companionship is what I impose.

Will enough of us begin to see that our fates are linked to allow mankind to survive and save us from our egotistical destructive actions on the earth? Am I an optimist or a pessimist about the future? I know I want to do my part, and since my attitude determines what I am open to, I *must* be an optimist. And each time I cherish an old friend and each time I open my heart and mind to a potential new one, I take the crucial first step towards the world I seek.

As I have grown older, I feel the connections with my friends more strongly. I have thought that one important reason is that Rita and I have no children of our own. However, I have observed that friends with many close and loving children feel the same. It also seems to be a characteristic of the later stages of life, when children are grown and independent. A hunger develops for the kinds of friendship we knew before the children arrived to occupy center stage.

I have not simply returned to an earlier developmental stage, however; there is a new mellow appreciation for the place of friends. It is an advance, a deepening of the awareness of connections with loved ones freely chosen. Friendships are cherished as never before, and as life begins to fade, they become a vehicle for the sometimes nearly desperate search for the meaning of it all. We nurture friends, for through them we can glimpse the hope that there may be a coherent affiliation beyond this mundane place.

So we call our friends more frequently, try to be with them more often, cautiously depend more on them. If we have lived away, we may move back to where our good friends remained, and secretly we think, as did Thomas Fuller, "May it please God not to make our friends so happy as to forget us!"

There is no reason to keep the secret, because we all seek an alliance of love that transcends the individual. Call it life's meaning, call it God, call it anything you like. We would, if we knew how, unite with it. And, in moments of synchrony with loving friends, we behold what it is like, a universal sacred moment here on earth.

TWENTY

Some Afterthoughts

Oh the comfort, the inexpressible comfort of feeling safe with a person: having neither to weigh thoughts nor measure words, but to pour them out. Just as they are—chaff and grain together, knowing that a faithful hand will take and sift them, keep what is worth keeping, and then with the breath of kindness, blow the rest away.

—GEORGE ELIOT

I ASKED many of my friends to write their perspectives on our friendships. I sent them what I had written, wondering how our versions might compare. And there begins a tale.

It was asking much too much of them, I realize now. But once begun, I had to see it through. Most first sent me testimonials . . . not words which would enlighten the meanings of friendship. I thanked them for their generosity, but explained that a testimonial was not my goal. Rather, I wanted them to describe a candid, more balanced view, which put a terrible imposition on their time and busy lives.

But they all came through, perhaps the ultimate tribute to their loyalty. Many of these descriptions went back and forth between us many different times, and in the process issues that were unresolved were exposed. For a time I feared I might lose some friends, as irritation surfaced. I was afraid I might unwittingly have even sacrificed a friend or two to write of them—what an irony that would have been, and certainly no tribute to friendship.

And yet, in the end, the conflicts were resolved, and increased the breadth and depth of our relationships. Some issues between friends are usually unknowingly skirted to preserve the harmony, and that had been the case. The resolutions often did not mean agreement, as much as a new appreciation of our differences.

Openness is not necessarily a virtue in itself. But in people with commitment and goodwill, the less hidden, the stronger the bond. So, as wrenching as it was, no friends were lost, and bonds were strengthened.

I incorporated some of what I learned into the text that comes before; however, the divergence and sometimes surprising similarity in view is often fascinating. The discrepancies in description between good friends prove that friendship is known primarily in ways beyond mere words, and no matter how elegantly they may have been selected, they can only hint at what the bonds really are.

So the responses of my friends are offered here to help us all discover more of the mysteries of being and having friends.

My Friends' Perspectives

BIG JIM: I accept without qualification whatever Arnie wishes to say about our early and present friendship, if it helps him characterize the bonding process. And that even includes what he said about my own bluntness and tactlessness. But the fact remains that a single chapter fails to describe a brotherhood that stretches, with few interruptions, across fifty years.

We do have different views about the beginning of our friendship. From my perspective, I first saw him when he sat two rows in back of me in high school, and seemed open to friendship. I was pleased, for he was an attractive but unassuming peer—athletic, unusually intelligent, ever-smiling, and slightly reserved. My admiration grew as I recognized how remarkable and versatile he really was. He excelled academically, and was artistically inclined in art and music, and I especially appreciated his ever-present warmth and humor.

We became high school best friends; I had a brotherly feeling towards him. My real brother was three years older, and we were never together in the same school at the same time.

The fact that Arnie had certain self-doubts in the puberty years only meant that he was like many of us at that age. I clearly recall celebrating our 1943 high school graduation at Earl Carroll's Nightclub in Hollywood with Arnie, Dick Reid, and Kenny Gabriel—four poor souls in search of womankind. We shared information about our clumsy maneuvers with girls, and our naivete lasted until college and navy years.

My mother was always aggressively involved with me; it worked out okay, and I was no doubt the same way later with my own children. Although popularity with peers was insignificant to her, it *was* important to me, probably because I heard so much at home about how "unimportant" it was to be one of the in crowd. I thought Arnie had it, while I didn't. After all, he was a Greek service-club president, and I was never invited to join. He helped me bridge the gap through personal encouragement and devotion to our relationship. He seemed to know how an outsider felt—and I learned that I could control my own destiny as time went on.

I was married to Phyllis in 1950, the year Arnie was hit with polio, and our friendship matured and changed somewhat because of it. Great distances intervened for many years. Nevertheless, we always talked on the phone or had short visits whenever we passed through the area. Keeping in touch was important to me, because I continued to feel a brotherly commitment. We returned to southern California in 1984, and then I could meet with him more frequently.

My recollections are subordinated to the broader emergence of Arnold, the man. To be sure, the onset of polio was tragic, but his forty paralyzed years since then are replete with professional and personal achievements and indeed many might not have occurred without this excruciating adversity. He "overcame" in every sense of the word.

Regardless of the individual in a pair of friends, there is a selfish, or self-centered gain in it for each, or it would never form. If the self-satisfaction is beneficial to the other individual, all the better, and the friendship endures. Maybe this is the way one should go into friendship—that way it is more likely to remain a satisfying relationship, and survive crises.

So, what do I get out of this relationship? For one thing, I feel as if I bet on the right horse in taking Arnie as my friend. How he has lived his life is vindication of my good judgment.

Having this great friend reaffirms my life, and I still find sustenance and strength in the support Arnie unfailingly gives. As we enter the "Indian summer" years, I expect the passage to be buoyed by my lifelong friend, and I hope I can do as much for him. If true greatness can be seen among the living, then I have seen it in him.

MARTY: My first recollection of Arnie is my seventh birthday party, which he attended because our parents were acquainted. Until a recent move, an enlargement of a picture from the party adorned my dressing room wall. What I mainly recall from that time was his self-assurance and generous smile.

My next memories are from sports, in which he was

always graceful. I admired his skills, and knowing we were both Jewish gave me a sense of pride. When we entered junior high, we played on the same teams, and I remember him as being a committed competitor, with quite a temper when things did not go his way.

Arnie had a wry sense of humor, sometimes tinged with sarcasm. I think he sometimes intimidated people, as he would "showboat" with dazzling verbal footwork. He was a star, and I saw him as Jack Armstrong, the All-American Boy, athletic and multitalented.

Yet when I was elected over him for junior high school judge, I felt no triumph. I never liked petty competitiveness when I heard it in my family, and it was not a part of me.

I was in law school in San Francisco when I read in the sports page of the *Chronicle,* "Arnold Beisser stricken with polio." I was stunned in disbelief: It could not be. Reports that appeared about him from time to time left a cloudy picture in my mind. It was not until a few years later, when visiting him in the hospital, that I discovered how severely he had been hit. It was a shock.

Our first connection was because we were Jewish. I learned great pride in that identity from my large extended family, while Arnie's small nuclear family gave him a sense of separation because of it. His ambivalence about it kept me outside his orbit, and I resented that. I wanted to be his friend, but he kept me out, so we traveled different, although parallel, roads.

I was envious of his many abilities, but I had mixed

feelings about him. It hurt that Jewishness, about which I felt pride, was what kept us apart. I felt he was someone I might have counted on as a friend, but he seemed unreachable and aloof. It was a loss for me, and my own remoteness kept me from being more understanding. Perhaps if I had been, our friendship would not have been so strained and awkward in our youth.

Our relationship is very different today, and we have a sensitive and everlasting friendship now. Arnie is different too. Although he has retained his talents, his sense of humor no longer has barbs. To call him my friend is one of the riches in my life, and I consider him an important member of my family. Even though we have talked of everything by now, I continually look forward to our meetings, where each time we grow closer, and each intimacy creates greater depths of understanding. That we have known each other so long, and endured so many trials and misreadings, has greatly strengthened our bond. And aren't we fortunate to have each other for the rest of our lives?

JERRY: Our friendship is now in its forty-third year, and when I think of Arnie, I have feelings of "oneness," like we came from the same egg, or that we are brothers from the same family.

What I am left with is a wonderful collection of "heart prints," more visceral than cognitive memories. These emotional recollections are beyond the limits of a description in words. I have a "heart print" of wonderful Saturday afternoons we spent with our friends drinking beer at Pop Risotti's, just outside the Stanford campus. I have a "heart print" of the terror we endured together as we went into a final examination, uncertain of whether we would pass or not.

His perceptions of our medical school days brought on a lot of tears and pain. I remembered my feelings of inadequacy, but I had repressed the magnitude of the feelings of loneliness and my longing to be accepted by others. I remember my envy at his easy way of communicating with the opposite sex, and his wonderful sense of humor. I also appreciated his tolerating my being on the same tennis court as him—when we both knew that he could always beat me, love and love.

One of the most painful and difficult experiences of my life was when I first saw him after he had come down with polio. I didn't want to look at his body, and I was afraid that he was going to die. I was scared to death that this could happen to me, and I felt guilty that I was well, and he was sick. I felt impotent to be helpful, and frustrated that I did not have a magic wand to fix him up and put him back in the same extraordinary physical shape he was in before. Painful as it was, I learned to look at his withered body . . . and then later to look beyond it to see only the light that had always been there.

Perhaps what is most valuable about our relationship is that it has made me feel free and loved. In our friendship I have always felt it was okay for me to be myself; I don't have to wear costumes with him, for he has seen me at my worst, and still loved and accepted me. I know in the deepest part of my being that any time I would be in need, he would be there to respond with love and acceptance, not judgments.

He has also been a wonderful teacher to me—not to feel sorry for myself, never to give up, to always persevere, knowing that there can always be a solution.

There is nothing we have not talked about with each other—politics, sex, family problems, sports, religion, death, life, and spiritual journeys. I have admired him, and cherish that we are trusted friends, who can fully communicate with each other and understand each other, very often without any words being passed back and forth.

If there is one word that summarizes our friendship for me, it is "gratefulness"—gratefulness that he is my friend, gratefulness for accepting my love and friendship, and for continuing to be there to spur me on to further growth in this journey we call life. As always, forever and forever, beyond all kinds of words, I love him, and my love will always be with him. I thank him for being who he is, and for loving me the way that he does.

TED: Although the automobile accident Arnie described had been on his mind for more than thirty years, I have no memory of it whatsoever. I've even forgotten the conversation of only a few years ago, in which he told me about it.

I am now sixty-five years old, and one might attribute

my forgetting to age. However, my memory is very good, but I have an extraordinary propensity to selectively forget events and conversations, or parts of conversations, if at the time they seem to me to be relatively insignificant.

When Arnie told me of the "event" that occurred so many years ago, I failed to appreciate how significant it had been for him. Perhaps I was aware of its importance to him, but since I had played an important role with my ill-concealed anger, I might have felt guilty. This certainly would be a very sound and reasonable psychological explanation for again forgetting.

When I first learned of Arnie's illness—probably within a year or two after it occurred—I would from time to time think about him. I also talked about him to friends, describing to them what I had heard from others of his remarkable adaptation to his disability. I was impressed by his success both in his work and in his relations with others. Although I liked and admired him in our student days because he was friendly, fun-loving, and an excellent tennis player, my admiration now was of a different order. It was based on what I recognized in the friend I never saw or spoke to: his courage, his wisdom, and his generosity.

Although I had a growing family and a busy practice, both of which commanded my attention, these were not the reasons I did not contact Arnie in the thirty-five intervening years. It had more to do with the fact that my life had gone so well, and his had been so difficult. Even though I was at first unaware that he was sick, I also felt guilty that I had not helped.

As the years went by it became increasingly difficult to renew our friendship. How would he react to my apparent indifference, I wondered? Would he be jealous of me and the life I had lived? These were the concerns that stood in my way. After I read an article he had published, I finally did call, for I think it was a signal that he was all right. Although ostensibly it was about the importance of the article, I needed to make the phone call and rekindle the friendship that had lain dormant for so many years.

It's interesting and terribly unfortunate that both Arnie and I experienced ourselves for so many years as betraying the other. Guilt had separated us. And if it were not for the fortuitous event of the article he wrote, we never would have known what happened, and we wouldn't have the friendship we now enjoy.

BALTIMORE BOB: At the age of six, our youngest son Adam began insisting on knowing who my best friend was. For years he would ask: "Is your best friend Eddie, Bill, Carl, Gene, or Arnie?" He would get me to elaborate on each, and why I saw them as a good friend. It was difficult to answer, for with each friend I experienced warmth, respect, and loyalty that has grown over the years.

I have had the good fortune of maintaining a few good friends from my elementary school and the neighborhood where I was reared. Others came from military service and workplaces during my forty years of employment. What has become clear now, but what I was unable to articulate to my son, is that each is a good friend, and to declare one as "best friend" would be more self-deception than reality.

Arnold Beisser has supplied me with a unique friendship. Ours is the noncombative, noncompetitive peer relationship that I always cherished, yet only had in fantasy. In my childhood, competition and winning were of paramount importance; however, even more important was the denial of them. "Compete until you drop, but don't let anyone know you feel competitive" was the family message.

Before I met Arnie, I had never met a man with whom I did not feel competitive. The paradox is that Arnie has also been a fiercely competitive man. Perhaps his pleasant voice, his warm smile and eyes removed the feeling of competition. It may have been because he was in a wheelchair, or that he seemed so dependent on the competent woman who is his wife, Rita. Or perhaps it was all these. But whatever it may have been, I felt safe and comfortably secure with Arnie, and did not need to guard against a fantasy of threat. A warmth and feelings of respect, joy, and mutual concern were immediate.

Over the seven or eight months when we first worked together, we communicated with humor, sincerity, warmth, openness, and mutual acceptance. I felt no need to perform. From the comfort of feeling safe has now grown unconditional acceptance and a deep love for each other.

Although for most of our twenty-four-year friendship we have lived a continent apart, our relationship has helped me to be more open to experience love, caring, warmth, concern, pain, and humor. When I think of Arnold Beisser, a special feeling rolls through me—that our lives will transcend this world, and is for eternity.

HELEN O: On reading what Arnie wrote about me, I was struck by how similar our memories are. He described the very same things I would have, and in much the same way. Nevertheless, I have two other recollections to add.

One has to do with my giving up smoking. I told only four people what I was doing; Arnie was one of them. I was afraid if I talked about it too much, I might substitute words for actually doing it. I wasn't sure I could quit smoking, but whether I did or not, I knew that he would be there for me, and support me whatever happened. That knowledge gave me additional strength and courage to do what I knew I should.

The other memory is of a birthday luncheon Arnie took me to at a local Szechuan Chinese restaurant. Because of my early life in Asia, I love hot spicy foods. Arnie let me order the hottest items on the menu. With tears streaming down my face, I remember telling him how delicious it was, and how appreciative I was. We laughed uproariously together at the irony of my combination of tears and pleasure. That was a part of the fun.

I have had a suffusion of warm feeling reading his comments about our friendship, and in remembering things we did together. The luxury of reliving and thinking over "old times" in this context has given me much joy. What Arnie does not mention at all or significantly underplays is his contribution and part in the creation of our friendship.

When I first met him and then began working with him, I was at a low point in my self-esteem. His confidence in me nurtured my positive feelings about myself until my strength returned. And I knew his interest and concern were not just professional, but very personal. He can be very critical, but the criticism is more positive than negative. He expects the best of those who work with him, and that expectation can *bring out* the best in people. That became one of the strongest links in forging a lasting friendship.

Although I agree love is an essential part of friendship, of no less importance is respect and trust, and I clearly felt them with him. Yes, he had his ideas and we had our differences, but they were always directed to our work together—not at or against me as a person. He says he has not seen my dark side, and there surely is one, but that is because I've never felt attacked or rejected by him. I did not need to defend myself or protect my integrity by showing my "darker" ways. Major themes in my life have been fear of abandonment and loss of love, but with Arnie they were rarely manifested.

When we first began to work together, I was in awe of

him. One winter, when he was ill with the flu, he let his beard grow. It was like Freud's, and very attractive to me. He wore it for many months. Then, one morning I arrived at work, and his beard was gone. I felt I had lost a god, and there he was, just an ordinary person. That was important in my growth, from reliance on someone superhuman to greater self-reliance. I no longer seemed to need a superman, but found that in Arnie becoming ordinary, he was a super person.

Although we had become good friends before my retirement, that event removed the barrier of his being the boss, for suddenly he wasn't anymore. A purer love and friendship could then emerge with him, and increasingly with Rita. How blessed I feel now to know both of them and be part of their lives. To them, I say, *Jag alskar dej.*

HUGH: The entire acquaintanceship between Arnie and me has been on the phone, with a little mail thrown in. As a consequence, I do not know his mannerisms or what he looks like and cannot react to even his physical disabilities. This I count as a blessing when I realize how many likes and dislikes of people have been nudged along by my reaction to their bodies as opposed to their souls. Nor has our relationship been affected by my seeing how he interacts with others. I don't know if he under-tips or over-tips in a restaurant, or if he even goes to them. I don't know how he reacts to spills, smells, interruptions, or noises. I don't know how he treats Rita or how she treats him. I don't know what to expect from him in business dealings.

Many people would consider these absences to be minor tragedies, but I don't because I have experienced his heart and want nothing else from him. I know his goodness because nothing blocks the view. I can't talk to him for more than a few minutes without beginning to feel the peace of God—and I don't even know his position on God!

In recent years I have managed to switch most of my counseling to the phone for similar reasons: My eyes can't get in the way of what I sense and what I need to hear the other person say; likewise, how I impress others physically does not interfere with what I want to say to them. Obviously, there are numerous disadvantages to relating over the phone. It would be hard to have children that way, although I'm sure they'll work it out through fiber optics. Also, not all people allow their real self to come through in speech alone, although it's surprising how many do.

I feel there is a very important lesson for me in my relationship with Arnie, and that if I could somehow learn it completely, I would never judge another human being. And wouldn't that be a relief. Clearly the lesson has nothing to do with the telephone. Rather, it is a matter of focus. What do I choose to focus on with this individual?—for there is indeed much to choose from. It is like picking out a lovely strain of music one hears while walking down a noisy street. Each person has that music within. And it *can* be heard. It's just that with Arnie, very little effort was required because I had before me a full orchestra.

ROSE: Arnie is correct that I do not use the word "friend" casually, and there are not many people who qualify. To say "my friend" has great meaning for me, and although he has been my boss, my teaching colleague, and my student, what pleases me most is that we are, indeed, friends.

I remember my first impressions of him and of the possibility of our working together as colleagues. His gentle warmth and giving character made me optimistic that we could work together as real colleagues. Without those qualities nothing would have developed, for I might not trust myself to whatever a joint relationship would bring.

The give-and-take in our relationships was energizing and unusual. What joy I found in our discussions of the acceptable differences in feelings. And I am very pleased that he has learned from me, for he is the kind of person I have always admired and, in my experience, not many such thoughtful men would give this compliment.

I have always taken myself too seriously, particularly in my later years, and what I treasure most is his helping me to take things more lightly. Through him I have gained greater acceptance of myself, and can more fully accept the completeness of nature, even when inexplicable. He has helped me appreciate the whole of life, and to accept that both life and death are essential parts.

How hard it is to satisfactorily express what our relationship has meant to me. But I can say he is my friend in the fullest sense of that word.

BUD: When Arnie and I first met three years ago, it was clear that we had a lot in common. For starters, we are the same age, we caught polio about the same time, and while Arnie suffered more severe paralysis than I, we are both confined to our respective wheelchairs, and we are both dependent on respirators for sleep.

We began to know each other through our early talks about the routines and equipment upon which our lives depend. Soon, we began talking to one another on an almost daily basis and, as contact turned to friendship, I sensed that I had, for the first time, found someone in a strikingly similar condition to my own with whom I could talk openly about even the most forbidding things we must both face. I had found in Arnie the disabled soul brother I never had.

From this growing closeness some differences also emerged. Arnie is a teacher, an author, and a highly decorated psychiatrist still in active practice. I am a retired businessman, having founded and managed my own company for twenty-eight years until it was sold in 1984. While Arnie admires my accomplishments, he has somewhat of an aversion to the business of business, as well as to some other topics of interest to me, one of which is my concern for his declining health. For reasons then unknown to me, he simply refused to discuss it with me, since, as he explained, there was nothing I could do about it anyway. This led me to become very frustrated, as I felt I was being denied expression of my concern. Some feisty exchanges followed.

Were these the first cracks in our friendship, or was this just a normal cycle? As I reflected on this, my attention turned from our differences back to the many needs, standards, and values we shared. I thought about how much comfort and reassurance I drew from our frequent phone conversations, how important Arnie had become to me, and how much I genuinely cared about him.

I decided to make a deliberate effort to explore our differences, to see if they could be resolved through discussion and better understanding. Some, including the "How are you?" problem, yielded to explanations that Arnie had not given me before, and some may never be reconciled, but my friendship with Arnie was preserved and strengthened by the process, and I was reminded that in friendship, as in other of life's endeavors, commitment can often transcend problems.

I cannot identify all the basic elements of our friendship. I know I was initially attracted to Arnie by our similar conditions, common interests, mutual goals, and the sharpness of his mind and wit. Then there is kinship, comfort, companionship, and the countless little things that happen—like the sharing of a silent laugh—as can best be appreciated between two breathless people like ourselves.

Whatever it is that brought us to where we are, of one thing I am sure. Arnie is my friend.

FRANK: The friendship between Doc and me has been more important to me in my life than to him in his. This statement in no way disparages our relationship, nor does it suggest any unhealthy imbalance. It simply reflects the differences in wisdom and maturity between us throughout our friendship. These differences have naturally influenced the character of our friendship.

I was a happy-go-lucky twenty-three-year-old, entering graduate school and needing a cheap place to live, when chance cast me upon Doc and Rita's hospitable doorstep. I was at the time possessed of little purpose, direction, or seriousness. I earned my keep by assisting Doc in rather intimate circumstances for twelve or so hours each week. I bathed him, shaved him, stretched him, and helped him go to the bathroom, among other things. Meanwhile we would talk, at first about safe general topics, then about more serious personal things. A relationship sprouted, although for me it was a rather confusing relationship. I began to see Doc as a mentor, a father, a buddy, even as I was, in fact, a hired hand. What was I to make of such a relationship with this wiser, more worldly person? How did he view me? Was I presumptuous to think that we were becoming friends?

Over time it became clear that indeed we had become friends. For me there was friendship, and more. I came of age during the two years I lived with Doc and Rita. I learned from them how to live with a sense of joy, purpose, and lighthearted seriousness. I began to "form up" as an individual, to understand how I could make my place in the world. I joined their circle of kinship, and I learned the concept that family need not be limited to blood relatives. I changed considerably during those two years, and I cried the day I drove the U-Haul away from their home to start a career.

The eleven years since have been filled with changes—marriage, three kids, new jobs, and moves from California to Texas, to the Midwest, to the East Coast. The bonds of friendship now include five Woods and two Beissers. We have stayed in touch. Doc sends letters of gentle wisdom to the kids, some of which wisdom they understand now, more of which they will understand when they are older. Rita sends crazy "care packages." The kids tear open the packages with delight, then pester me and Charlotte to go to the store to assemble an equally crazy package to send back. We visit Doc and Rita as we are able. Their advice and wisdom help us to chart our course as we raise our family. Doc and Rita are points of reference in our sometimes chaotic little world. Our kids, when they grow up, will recall Doc and Rita as important characters in the story of their growing up.

We named our youngest child Arnie. Had he been a she, she would have been Rita. Little Arnie is twenty months old now, rapidly changing into a complex little individual. Although I love all three kids dearly, I must say that there seems to be an extra dimension, a certain poignancy, associated with little Arnie. I can't pin down exactly what this extra dimension is; I feel it, but I don't quite understand it. Maybe it is simply that he is our last child, and we know from our experience with our oldest child how precious these fleeting years of growing up are. Yet there must be something else.

A couple of weeks ago we made a pilgrimage from our home in the Midwest to southern California. A central purpose for the trip was to make the first in-person introduction of big Arnie to little Arnie. We visited Disneyland the day before we were to visit Doc and Rita. In the late morning, little Arnie, tired from the long trip and excitement of the morning, fell asleep in my arms as I sat in Tomorrowland. With his heart beating against mine and his quiet breathing in my ear, I sank into reverie.

I thought about the anticipation I had been feeling for the meeting of the Arnies, and about my recent preoccupation with delivering little Arnie to big Arnie rested and healthy, so that big Arnie could experience what a wonderful little guy little Arnie is. I thought about the excitement the entire family had been feeling for the past several weeks, as we counted down the days to our visit. My mind went back to the time I had lived with Doc and Rita, rehashing old scenes and images.

As I held little Arnie in my arms, I thought of the many times I had held big Arnie in my arms, carrying him to and from bed, and bath, and wheelchair, and car. A powerful image came suddenly to me. I imagined for a moment that the two Arnies, the one in my arms now and the one in my arms years ago were but one, and that I was the link that connected them. I became emotional and misty-eyed as I contemplated this image. I wanted to wipe away the tears, but to move my arms might disturb Arnie, who needed to be just right for his meeting tomorrow. So I sat quietly amid the hubbub of Tomorrowland with tears running down my cheeks, the little guy snoring lightly on my shoulder, wondering at the mysteries of friendship and parenthood.

I Get the Last Word

How fascinating it is to me that Frank began his note by saying that our friendship was more important to him than to me. But candor begets candor, and I have known before that I dared not admit how important his friendship has been for me. I did not want to let on that my visit with Frank, his family, and especially little Arnie, fulfilled an uncompleted part of my life.

Why should I have been so hesitant about openly declaring this? Pride . . . and that I might feel embarrassed that Frank and his family meant so much to me, if I meant less to them. How foolish such false pride is.

Yet it is the very reason friendships are destroyed or never allowed to grow beyond a superficial plane—fear of loss of face, of being foolish, of being weak, vulnerable, or taken advantage of—they keep us from enjoying this most vital of connections. So we are more apt to keep countless superficial friends, rather than entering into depth with one who counts.

I am not related to the Wood family, I thought, so how dare I assume the intimate privileges of family. They have their own parents, grandparents, aunts, and uncles, so how, I thought, could I presume that Rita and I were just as close to them. But now, seeing the error in my ways, I do declare that Frank and Charlotte, Nathan, Marianne and Arnie are my kin, and I love them all.

I say thank you to all my other friends as well. You have made my life complete. And thank you, Frank, for the last of these responses from my friends, for in what you wrote, many of the most remarkable qualities of friendship are clearly summarized. Your thoughts of big and little Arnies, connected as though one, transcending both time and space, reveals that through true friendships we can all enter into the realm of eternity.